RESOLUTIONS

PASSED BY THE

TRUSTEES OF COLUMBIA COLLEGE;

FROM

1868 to 1874.

NEW YORK:
D. VAN NOSTRAND, Nos. 23 MURRAY AND 27 WARREN ST.

1874.

CONTENTS.

	PAGE
Board of Trustees	7
Standing Committee	8
Committee on Course of Instruction	8
Committee on the School of Mines	8
Committee on the School of Law	9
Committee on the Library	9
Committee on Honors	9
Accumulating Fund	13
Admission	14
Appropriation	14
Attendance	23
College Discipline	23
Commencements and Exhibitions	24
Chemistry, Department of	24
Degrees	25
Diplomas	25
Examinations	25
Fees	27
Fellowships	29
Financial Policy, permanent	30
Gebhard Fund	31
Herbarium	32
Instruction, Committee on Course of	33
Library	39
Medicine, School of	112
Meteorological Observations	41

CONTENTS.

	PAGE
Mines, School of	92
Miscellaneous	39
Observatory, Astronomical	40
Ordinance, establishing a permanent financial policy	113
President, of the	40
Printing	41
Prize Scholarships and Prizes	42
Professorships and Professors	44
Repairs	50
Rowing	51
Salaries	52
Scholarships, free	58
Seal	56
Site, Committee on the	59
Statutes, Committee on the	62
Standing Committee	68
Students	80
Treasurer	80
Trustees	86
Tutorships	91
Errata	118

COLUMBIA COLLEGE.

BOARD OF TRUSTEES.

NAMES.	RESIDENCES.
HAMILTON FISH, LL. D., Chairman of the Board	251 East 17th Street.
SAMUEL B. RUGGLES, LL. D	24 Union Square,
WM. BETTS, LL. D, Clerk	122 East 30th Street.
BENJAMIN I. HAIGHT, S. T. D., LL. D	56 West 26th "
ROBERT RAY	363 West 28th "
GOUVERNEUR M. OGDEN, Treasurer	187 Fulton, h. 84 West 11th "
HENRY J. ANDERSON, M. D., LL. D	60 Park Avenue.
EDWARD L. BEADLE, M. D	Poughkeepsie.
GEORGE T. STRONG	113 East 21st Street.
MANCIUS S. HUTTON, S. T. D	47 East Ninth "
HORATIO POTTER, S. T. D., LL. D., D. C. L	38 East 22d "
LEWIS M. RUTHERFURD	175 Second Avenue.
THOMAS DE WITT, S. T. D	55 East Ninth Street.
JOHN C. JAY, M. D	Rye, or 24 West 48th "
WILLIAM C. SCHERMERHORN	49 West 23d "
MORGAN DIX, S. T. D	27 West 25th "
FREDERICK A. P. BARNARD, S. T. D., LL. D., L. H. D.,	College Green.
SAMUEL BLATCHFORD, LL. D	12 West 22d Street.
STEPHEN P. NASH	11 West 19th "
CHARLES R. SWORDS	156 Broadway.
ANTHONY HALSEY	291 Broadway.
JOSEPH W. HARPER	231 Pearl Street.
CORNELIUS R. AGNEW, M. D.	244 Madison Avenue.
EVERT A. DUYCKINCK	20 Clinton Place.

COMMITTEES OF THE TRUSTEES.

STANDING COMMITTEE.

NAMES.	RESIDENCES.
GOUVERNEUR M. OGDEN, Chairman	84 West 11th Street.
WILLIAM BETTS, LL. D.	122 East 30th "
CHARLES R. SWORDS.	156 Broadway.
WILLIAM C. SCHERMERHORN	40 West 23d Street.
ANTHONY HALSEY	291 Broadway.
JOSEPH W. HARPER	231 Pearl Street.

COMMITTEE ON THE COURSE OF INSTRUCTION.

NAMES.	RESIDENCES.
HORATIO POTTER, S. T. D., LL. D., D. C. L.	38 East 22d Street.
MORGAN DIX, S. T. D.	27 West 25th "
GEORGE T. STRONG	113 East 21st "
LEWIS M. RUTHERFURD	175 Second Avenue.
FREDERICK A. P. BARNARD, S. T. D., LL. D., L. H. D.,	College Green.

COMMITTEE ON THE SCHOOL OF MINES.

NAMES.	RESIDENCES.
WILLIAM BETTS, LL. D., Chairman	122 East 30th Street.
GEORGE T. STRONG	113 East 21st "
LEWIS M. RUTHERFURD	175 Second Avenue.
FREDERICK A. P. BARNARD, S. T. D., LL. D., L. H. D.,	College Green.
HAMILTON FISH, LL. D.	251 East 17th Street.

COMMITTEE ON THE SCHOOL OF LAW.

NAMES.	RESIDENCES.
SAMUEL B. RUGGLES, LL. D., Chairman	24 Union Square.
HAMILTON FISH, LL. D.	251 East 17th Street.
GOUVERNEUR M. OGDEN, Esq.	84 West 11th "
GEORGE T. STRONG, E·q.	113 East 21st "
WILLIAM BETTS, LL. D.	122 East 30th "
SAMUEL BLATCHFORD, LL. D.	12 West 22d "
STEPHEN P. NASH	11 West 19th "
THEODORE W. DWIGHT, LL. D.	8 Great Jones "

COMMITTEE ON THE LIBRARY.

NAMES.	RESIDENCES.
HENRY J. ANDERSON, M. D., LL. D., Chairman	60 Park Avenue.
GEORGE T. STRONG	113 East 21st Street.
WILLIAM C. SCHERMERHORN	49 West 23d "
FREDERICK A. P. BARNARD, S. T. D., LL. D., L. H. D., College Green.	
BENJAMIN I. HAIGHT, S. T. D., LL. D.	56 West 26th Street.
BEVERLEY R. BETTS, Clerk	122 East 30th "

COMMITTEE ON HONORS.

NAMES.	RESIDENCES.
WILLIAM BETTS, LL. D., Chairman	122 East 30th Street.
HORATIO POTTER, S. T. D., LL. D., D. C. L.	38 East 22d "
HENRY J. ANDERSON, M. D., LL. D.	60 Park Avenue.
GEORGE T. STRONG	113 East 21st Street.
FREDERICK A P. BARNARD, S. T. D., LL. D., L. H. D., College Green.	

RESOLUTIONS

OF THE

TRUSTEES OF COLUMBIA COLLEGE.

ACCUMULATING FUND.

<small>1868, Nov. 2.
Accumulating Fund.</small>   *Resolved*, That ten thousand seven hundred and eighty-five dollars and eighty-one cents, being the balance of cash remaining at the end of the last financial year, be appropriated and set apart as a part of the accumulating fund.

<small>1869, Nov. 1.
Accumulating Fund.</small>   *Resolved*, That two thousand, five hundred and thirty dollars and twelve cents, surplus income for the financial year last past, be appropriated and set apart for the accumulating fund.

<small>1870, Nov. 1.
Amount set apart for Accumulating Fund.</small>   *Resolved*, That from the surplus income of the last preceding year, shall be appropriated and set apart for the accumulating fund, the cash balance of \$8,877.06, the investment of \$10,912.50 in stock of the State of New York, and \$10,000 deposited with the New York Life Insurance and Trust Company, with the interest accrued on the last named amount.

<small>1871, June 5.
Award to College Park place extension.</small>   *Resolved*, That eighty-six thousand five hundred dollars, the amount of the award made to the college in the matter of the extension of Park Place, be added to the accumulating fund.

<small>1871, Nov. 6.
Accumulating Fund.</small>   *Resolved*, That the following appropriations be made to the accumulating fund :

1. Of the surplus increase of the year ending on the 30th September, 1871, consisting of the following items:

    Cash balance on 30th September, 1871.... $5,721 99
    Deposit on interest................................ 12,000 00
    Invested.. 1,849 36

                                                                                                $19,571 35

together with all interest accrued thereon.

2. Of the amount expected to be received for the commutations of rents, reserved in grants, in fee of certain lots of land now owned by the estate of William Rhineander, deceased, $7,431.80.

1872, Nov. 4. Accumulating Fund.   *Resolved*, That the whole amount remaining to the credit of the accumulating fund be applied to the loan which, by resolutions of this Board, passed on twenty-second day of October, 1872, the Committee on the Site was authorized to direct to be made upon mortgage of land, to be provisionally secured for the future site of the college.

ADMISSION.

1868, June 1. Requirements for entering Freshman Class.   *Resolved*, That the resolution of the board of the college, that there be hereafter required for admission to the Freshman Class four books of Legendre's Geometry, be approved, and that the recommendation that there be required for admission as above, in connection with arithmetic, a knowledge of the metric system of weights, measures and moneys, be also approved, with the understanding that such conditions shall not be enforced until the examinations of June, 1870.

APPROPRIATION.

1868, June 1. Cases for Prof. Peck's room.   *Resolved*, That a sum not exceeding one hundred dollars be appropriated for constructing cases for the apparatus in Professor Peck's room.

APPROPRIATION.

1868, Nov. 2.
Appropriation Department of Mining Engineering.
Resolved, That the sum of five hundred dollars be appropriated for the improvement of apparatus, &c., in the department of mining engineering, for the current academic year.

1858, Nov. 2.
Appropriation for furniture.
On motion of the president, *Resolved*, That the sum of fifty dollars be appropriated for the purpose of renewing, so far as may be necessary, the furniture in the room occupied by the assistant of the professor of chemistry.

1869, Feb. 1.
Appropriation add. Physics.
Resolved, That a sum, not exceeding one hundred and fifty dollars, be appropriated, to be expended, under the direction of the president, for the construction of an additional case for the protection of the apparatus of the department of Physics, to be charged to "contingencies."

1869, April 5.
Sports and games
Resolved, That a sum not exceeding one hundred dollars be appropriated, to be used, under the direction of the president, to provide for and encourage the sports and exercises of the students in the open air.

1869, May 3.
Appropriations or 1869-70.
Resolved, That the following sums be appropriated for the several purposes stated for the use of the College and the School of Mines, for the financial year ending October 1, 1870.

COLLEGE.

Physics	$700	English Classics and Mathematics	$300
Mechanics	500	Library	2,000
Chemistry	300	Supplies	1,500
Geodesy	400	Sports and Games	100
Botany	500		

SCHOOL OF MINES.

Mineralogy	$500	Metallurgy	$500
Metal. Lab	250	Geology	500
Paleontology	500	Chemistry	4,000
Mining Engineering	500	Drawing	250
Civil Engineering	500	Library	2,000
Supplies	3,500	Printing and Advertising	2,500

APPROPRIATION.

Resolved, That the following sums be appropriated for the purposes stated, to be expended under the direction of the President.

1869, June 7. *Resolved,* That the sum of two hundred and fifty dollars be appropriated for the purpose of adding to the furniture of the president's house during the ensuing financial year.

1869, Nov. 1. Athletic sports. *Resolved,* That the sum of two hundred dollars be appropriated for the encouragement of athletic sports and games among the students, during the present year, to be expended under the direction of the president.

1869, Nov. 1. Appropriations. *Resolved,* That the appropriations heretofore made, for the financial year ending September 30, 1870, for the objects hereinafter named, be increased to the sums set opposite them respectively, viz. :

For Supplies for the college........from $1,500 to $2,000
" Printing and advertising...... " 1,500 " 2,000
"   "   "   "   S. of M. " 2,000 " 2,500
" Department of Minerals and Metallurgy :
"   Mineralogy..................from   500 "   750
"   Metallurgy................. "   500 "   750

Resolved, That a sum not exceeding fifty dollars be appropriated, in addition to the former appropriation, to the same object, for the purpose of defraying expenses of importation of articles purchased for the college, by the president, by authority of the trustees, in 1867.

1870, May 2 $80 to be paid Mr. Cummings. *Ordered,* That the sum of $80 be paid to Mr. Thomas P. Cummings to meet the expense of excavations in Lot L, 6, in Fiftieth street.

1870, May 2. Appropriations for the next academic year. *Resolved,* That the several sums be appropriated to the purposes hereinafter named for the maintenance of the operations of the College and School of Mines during the financial year commencing October 1, 1870, and ending September 3, 1871, viz.:

FOR THE COLLEGE.

Supplies	$2,000
Printing and Advertising	2,500
Library	2,000
Physics	500
Mechanics and Astronomy	500
Chemistry	500
English and Classical	300
Commencement	500
Societies	400
Sports and Games	200
Furniture for President's House	250
Botanical Library and Herbarium	500
Total	$10,150

SCHOOL OF MINES.

Supplies	$3,500
Printing and Advertising	2,500
Library	2,000
Foreign Fxchanges	1,000
Department of Analyt. Chemistry	4,000
" Mineralogy	750
" Metallurgy	750
Metallurgical Laboratory	500
Department of Civil Engineering	500
Department of Drawing	250
Examination of Smithsonian Minerals	50
Department of Geology	500
" Paleontology	500
Total	$16,800

1870, June 6. Supplies, special appropriation.   *Resolved,* That the sum of three thousand dollars be appropriated to meet the anticipated deficiency in the appropriation heretofore made for Supplies in the School of Mines.

1870, June 6. Cases, School of Mines, special appropriation.   *Resolved,* That a sum not exceeding three hundred dollars be appropriated for the purpose of procuring cases for the collection of objects illustrative of the applications of Chemistry, the same to be expended by the Professor of Analytical and Applied Chemistry under the direction of the President.

<small>1870, June 6.
Special appropriation, repairs.
School of Mines and College.</small>

Resolved, That the sum of three hundred dollars be appropriated for the purpose of making necessary repairs in the School of Mines, and also a further sum not exceeding two hundred dollars for repairs in the College, these said sums to be expended under the direction of the President.

<small>1870, June 6.
Special appropriation, repairs
Janitor's house.</small>

Resolved, That a sum not exceeding seventy-five dollars be appropriated for the purpose of procuring necessary repairs to be made to the house occupied by the Janitor, the same to be expended by said Janitor with the approval of the President.

<small>1870. June 6.
$200 advanced for purchases in Department of Geology, School of Mines.</small>

Resolved, That the Treasurer be authorized to advance to the Professor of Geology, &c., in the school of Mines, the sum of two hundred dollars on account of the appropriations made to the Departments of Geology and Paleontology for the ensuing financial year, the same to be expended under the direction of the Professor for the benefit of the collections belonging to said department during the present summer in Europe.

<small>1870, June 6.
Appropriation
Department of Physics.</small>

Resolved, That in lieu of the appropriation of five hundred dollars made at the last meeting of the Trustees for the use of the Department of Physics for the financial year ending September 30, 1871, there be appropriated seven hundred dollars to said department for the same year.

<small>1870, Nov. 7.
$1,500 added to appropriation for supplies.</small>

Resolved, That in addition to the appropriation heretofore made of two thousand dollars for the supplies of the college for the year commencing October 1, 1870, there be now appropriated the further sum of fifteen hundred dollars for the same object.

APPROPRIATION. 19

1871, May 1. *Resolved,* That there be appropriated for the maintenance of the College and the School of Mines during the the financial year commencing October 1st, 1871, the several sums hereinafter named, to be expended for the purposes specified respectively, viz.:

FOR THE COLLEGE.

Supplies	$3,000
Printing and advertising	2,500
Library	2,000
Physics	500
Mechanics and astronomy	500
Chemistry	500
English and classical department	300
Commencement	500
Societies	400
Furnishing President's house	250
Books, Library and Herbarium	500
Sports and games	200
	$11,050

FOR THE SCHOOL OF MINES.

Supplies	$3,500
Printing and advertising	2,500
Library	2,000
Analytical chemistry	4,000
Mineralogy	500
Metallurgy	500
Metallurgic laboratory	250
Mining engineering	500
Civil engineering	500
Drawing	350
Geology	500
Paleontology	500
	$16,600

1871, May 1. Balances on hand to be added to appropriations next year.

Resolved, That any balances which may remain unexpended at the close of the present financial year, of appropriations to the purposes hereinafter named, viz.: to the Library of the College, to the Department of Physics, of Mechanics and Astronomy, and of Chemistry, to the Botanical Library and Herbarium, and to the furnishing of the President's house, also to the Library of the School of Mines, to the Department of Analytical Chemistry, of Mineralogy, Metallurgy, and the Metallurgic Laboratory, of Mining and Civil Engineering and of Drawing, of Geology, and Paleontology, be carried forward and added to the appropriations for the same objects for the financial year ensuing.

1871, June 5.
Appropriation for repairs.

Resolved, That a sum not exceeding four hundred and twenty-five dollars be appropriated for the purpose of making, during the ensuing vacation, such repairs and changes in and about the college building and chapel as may be necessary, in anticipation of resumption of exercises in October next.

1871, June 5.
Safe to be bought

Resolved, That there be purchased a safe for the secure preservation of the original minutes of the Trustees of the College, and those of the Faculty, with the records of standing and attendance, and other papers of value, provided that the cost of the same shall not exceed three hundred dollars, and that it shall be paid out of the appropriation for supplies for the current academic year.

1871, June 5.
Amendment to ordinance, appropriation to Applied Chemistry.

The amendment to the ordinance establishing the permanent policy of the college, authorizing appropriation of $750 for applied chemistry, which was first considered and passed at a stated meeting on the first day of May last, was again considered and passed.

1871, June 5.
Appropriation to Applied Chemistry for 1871.

Resolved, That the sum of five hundred dollars be appropriated for the improvement of the collection and other means of instruction in Applied Chemistry during the academic year commencing October 1st, 1871, the same to be expended under the direction of the Professor of Analytical and Applied Cnemistry, with the approval of the President.

APPROPRIATION. 21

1871, Oct. 2.
Purchase carpet Trustees' room.
Resolved, That the Treasurer have authority to purchase a carpet and such other furniture as may be necesary for the Trustees' room.

1871, Nov. 6.
$600 for a safe.
Resolved, That a sum not exceeding six hundred dollars be appropriated for the purchase of a safe, to be placed in the President's room at the college, for the preservation of the original minutes of the Trustees, and the Faculty, and other valuable papers and books; the same to be in lieu of an appropriation of three hundred dollars heretofore made for a similar purpose.

1872, June 3.
President to be reimbursed $50.
Resolved, That the Treasurer be authorized to reimburse the President the sum of fifty dollars, expended by him over and above the amount allowed by permanent resolution, in order to secure the service of a secretary during the emergency occurring in December last.

1872, June 3.
$150, repairs for the School of Mines.
Resolved, That a sum not exceeding one hundred and fifty dollars be appropriated for the purpose of making such repairs as may be necessary in the building occupied by the School of Mines; the same to be expended under the direction of the President.

1872, Oct. 7.
Two hundred and twenty-five dollars and twenty-four cents appropriated for deficiency in School of Mines.
Resolved, That the sum of two hundred and twenty-five dollars and twenty-four cents be appropriated to meet a deficiency in the appropriation for supplies in the School of Mines for the year ending September 30th, 1872.

1872, Dec. 2.
$150 applied for tables in School of Mines.
Resolved, That the sum of one hundred and fifty dollars, or so much thereof as may be necessary, be appropriated to provide for the construction of new tables in the blowpipe laboratory of the School of Mines.

1873, Mar. 3.
Babcock's fire extinguishers.
Resolved, That the Treasurer be authorized, in his discretion, to purchase, for the use of the college, a number of Babcock's Fire Extinguishers, not exceeding ten.

APPROPRIATION.

1873, April 7.
Bill of Mr. Muller to be paid.

Resolved, That a bill of Martin Muller, painter, of forty-six dollars and fifteen cents, for repairs in the School of Mines, be paid.

1873, June 3.
Bill of J. W. Queen & Co. to be paid.

Resolved, That the Treasurer be authorized to pay the bill of J. W. Queen & Co. to the amount of 176\frac{25}{100}$, for a set of models of Descriptive Geometry, ordered for the use of the mathematical department.

1873, June 3.
$300 appropriated for English, Classical, and Mathematical Departments.

Resolved, That the title of the appropriation made at the last meeting of the Board, for the benefit of the English and Classical departments for the ensuing financial year, be altered so as to read English, Classical, and Mathematical; and that the amount of such appropriation be increased from two hundred dollars to three hundred dollars.

1873, June 3.
$175 appropriated for gas fixtures in School of Mines.

Resolved, That a sum not exceeding one hundred and seventy-five dollars be appropriated, to be expended under the direction of the President, for the purpose of introducing gas fixtures to illuminate the various apartments of the School of Mines for public evening receptions.

1873, Oct. 6.
Bill of A. T. Stewart & Co.

Resolved, That the action of the Treasurer in paying the bill of Messrs. A. T. Stewart & Co., for fitting a carpet to the room of the Trustees, amounting to 24\frac{75}{100}$, be approved.

Nov. 3.
Appropriations passed and laid over.

Resolved, That, in addition to the ordinary appropriations for the Department of Physics made for this year, and which may be made for the next, nine hundred dollars be appropriated for that department, to be applied for the purchase of a Gyroscope, of Nachet's new improved microscope, and of the Electro-dynamic Engine, such additional appropriation to be paid one-half during this financial year and one-half during the year next succeeding.

1873, Nov. 3.
Supplies.

Resolved, That the sum of $633.96 be appropriated to make good the deficiences in the appropriations for sup-

APPROPRIATION.   23

plies for the College and in the School of Mines, for the year ending September 30, 1873—to wit, $431.41 for the college and $202.55 for the School of Mines.

1873, Nov. 3. *Resolved*, That a sum, not exceeding $425, be appropri-
Room for Mathematical teacher ated to defray the expenses of repairing and furnishing
in School of a room for the Mathematical Department of the School
Mines. of Mines, and for introducing additional furniture and altering the arrangements in other departments for the accommodation of the increased number of students attending the school.

Repairs in School *Resolved*, That the sum of $150 be appropriated to
of Mines. defray the expense of repairing the chimneys and of a portion of the roof of the School of Mines.

ATTENDANCE.

1872, Oct. 7. *Resolved*, That the petition of Mr. R. B. Lloyd, a deaf
Mr. Lloyd excused from daily mute, who has been admitted to the Freshman Class, to
attendance. be excused from attendance on the daily exercise of the class, provided he attend and pass satisfactorily all the examinations monthly and quarterly, be granted.

COLLEGE DISCIPLINE.

1869, Dec. 20. *Resolved*, That in case it may be thought expedient by
Students not to the Faculty to modify the present regulations in regard
go out. to the egression of students from the lecture rooms, they be authorized to consider any student so egressing as not entitled to credit for attendance on the exercise from which such egression takes place.

COMMENCEMENTS AND EXHIBITIONS.

<small>1868, June 1.
Appropriation for Commencement.</small>   *Resolved,* That the sum of two hundred dollars, or so much thereof as may be necessary, be appropriated, in addition to the three hundred dollars appropriated by the standing resolution, to defray the necessary expenses of the annual Commencement.

<small>1869, Apr. 5.
Appropriation for Commencement</small>   *Resolved,* That the sum of two hundred dollars be appropriated, in addition to the standing annual appropriation of three hundred dollars, to the purpose of defraying the expenses of the Commencement in June next.

<small>1869, June 7.
Commencement expenses.</small>   *Resolved,* That one hundred dollars be appropriated to defray the expenses of the Commencement of the Law School, to be paid annually on the order of the warden of the school.

<small>1870, June 6.
Commencement.</small>   *Resolved,* That the sum of five hundred dollars be appropriated to defray the expenses of the ensuing Commencement, the same to be in lieu of the appropriation made by permanent resolution, and to be paid on the order of the President.

DEPARTMENT OF CHEMISTRY.

<small>1871, Oct. 2.
Hour allowed to Professor Joy.</small>   *Resolved,* That Professor Joy be authorized to occupy the hour heretofore allotted weekly with the Senior Class to the Lecturer on the Evidences of Religion, until the further order of this Board.

<small>1873, Mar. 3.
Leave to Prof. Joy to rent his house.</small>   *Resolved,* That with the approbation of the President of the College, Professor Joy be permitted to rent the house occupied by him, during such time as his family may be absent from the country; this permission not to extend beyond October 1st, 1874.

DEGREES.

1873, June 2. *Resolved*, That Otis Field, for three years a member of the Class of 1873 in good standing, who has been compelled, during the academic year 1872–3, to engage in teaching for his own support, and has thus been unable to continue his attendance during the year at college, be admitted to examination as a candidate for a degree of Bachelor of Arts, together with the class graduating in June, 1874, and that, if in that examination he be found qualified, he then receive that degree.

1873, Nov. 3.
Degrees to be conferred. *Resolved*, That the degrees of Bachelor and Master of Arts be conferred upon such candidates in course as shall be recommended by the Board of the College, and the degrees of Bachelor of Science and Engineer of Mines upon such students as shall be recommended by the Faculty of the School of Mines.

DIPLOMAS.

1870, May 2.
Law diplomas. *Resolved*, That the Warden of the Law School, whenever, in his opinion, the special circumstances of the case may require it, be authorized to deliver to any graduate the diploma certifying to such graduation before the Commencement exercises occur, and in anticipation of them.

EXAMINATIONS.

1869, Dec. 20
Composition to be taken into account in determining standing. *Resolved*, That whereas the exercises of composition and declamation are not matters capable of being properly included among the subjects of examination at the close of the collegiate sessions, the Faculty be authorized and instructed to give due weight to these exercises in the final determination of standing.

EXAMINATIONS.

1870, March 7.
Report of Committee on Statutes.

The Committee on the Statutes, to whom it was referred at the last meeting of the Board to consider and report upon the subject of alleged irregularities and improper proceedings at the examinations, and the best mode in their judgment to prevent the recurrence of the same, reported by their chairman, Dr. Haight, that they had given attention to the matter referred to them and conferred with the Faculty in regard to it, and that they have agreed to the following regulations in regard to the standing of the students and the conduct of their examinations:

Regulations.

1870, March 7.

1. Each Professor to report to the Board of the College at the end of every month, a numerical scale of the standing of all the students under his instruction, the order of merit to be determined in any way the Professor may choose.

2. The term examinations to be conducted in writing, in connection with such oral examination in each case as the Professor may deem necessary.

3. The attendance of the students to be obligatory and the Professors to have power to enforce recitations and to require a student where deficient to take a private tutor.

4. Gowns not to be worn at examinations.

5. The maximum for the term examination to be made equal to the sum of the monthly maxima. The standing of the students respectively to be determined according to the numerical values attained during the session according to the monthly reports and at the examination.

1871. January 9.
Senior Class Examination competition.

Resolved, That in awarding honors to the present Senior Class at the close of the year, the Board of the College be authorized to consider, along with the results of the competitive examination, the past record of the Scholarship of the Class, and also to confine the competitive examination to subjects taught during the Senior Year.

FEES. 27

1871, Feb. 6.
Honors to present Senior Class.
Resolved, That the present Senior Class be exempted from the operation of the provisions of Chapter VIII. of the Statutes, on competitive examinations for honors; and that honors be awarded in that class at the close of their academic course on the same principles as heretofore.

1871, Nov. 6.
Resolved, That hereafter, examinations in the Evidences shall be dispensed with, and that proficiency in this subject shall not be considered in making up the record of standing in scholarship.

1872, Nov. 4.
Honors.
Resolved, That the Board of the College be authorized, if in their judgment it shall be deemed expedient, to institute examinations for honors at the end of the Freshman, Sophomore, and Junior years, as well as at the end of the Senior year, such examinations to be conducted under the conditions heretofore prescribed for conducting the honor examinations of the Senior Class.

1872, Dec. 2.
Honor examinations in Junior, Sophomore and Freshman Classes.
Resolved, That the Board of the College be authorized, if in their judgment it shall be deemed expedient, to institute examinations for honors at the end of the Freshman, Sophomore, and Junior years, as well as at the end of the Senior year; such examinations to be conducted under the conditions heretofore prescribed for conducting the honor examinations of the Senior Class.

FEES.

1868, Oct. 5.
A. W. Frazer's case.
Resolved, That the sum of one hundred dollars, paid in October last by A. W. Frazer, of the present sophomore class, as his tuition fee for the academic year ending June 1868, during which year he was prevented from attendance at college by ill health, be accepted as applicable on account of his tuition for the present year, and that he be discharged from liability for tuition for the freshman year.

FEES.

The president offered a resolution as follows, viz.:

<small>1868, Nov. 2.
A. W. Frazer's case.</small> *Resolved,* That the treasurer be authorized to refund so much of the fee paid by A. W. Frazer in October, 1867, for tuition during the academic year ending in June last, during which he was prevented by illness from attending, as in the judgment of the president may appear to be equitable, which, upon his motion, was referred to a committee consisting of the president, the chairman of the board, and the treasurer, with instructions to report some general rule in relation to refunding fees.

<small>1869, Feb. 1.
Mr. Frazer.</small> *Ordered,* That the treasurer refund one-half of the tuition fee paid by Mr. Frazer.

At a meeting of the Law School Committee, January 23d, 1869:

<small>1869, Feb. 1.
Mr. Byrne.</small> *Resolved,* That it be recommended to the trustees to refund to Mr. ——— Byrne the amount of his tuition fee, he having attended the school but one day since entering it.

<small>1869, Feb. 1.
Gen. J. H. Bell.</small> *Resolved,* That it be recommended to the trustees to refund to Gen. John H. Bell one-half his tuition fee, on the ground that he is compelled to leave the school by the consequences of wounds received in service.

The recommendations of the committee were approved and the resolutions adopted.

<small>1870, Jan. 3.
$50 refunded to F. S. Jones.</small> *Resolved,* That the Treasurer be authorized to refund to Frank S. Jones, late a special student in the School of Mines, the sum of fifty dollars paid by him as a tuition fee.

<small>1870, Nov. 7.
To refund fee L. K. Miller.</small> *Resolved,* That the Treasurer be authorized to refund, on the order of the President, to Mr. Livingston K. Miller, the amount of the tuition fee of his son, I. Ernest Miller, who became a member of the class of 1873, in October last, but was prevented by permanent illness from attending at the college after the fifth day of October, 1869, which was the second day of the session.

1870, Nov. 7.
Tuition fee of Frank Storrs.

Resolved, That whereas Frank Storrs, a member of the class of 1873, was taken down with a painful disease of one of his limbs, in the month of October last, and was compelled to be absent during all the remainder of the academic year, and finally to fall back into the class of 1874, therefore the tuition fee paid by him in 1869 be accepted as payment in full for his tuition up to the end of the present year.

1871, Nov 6.
Fee F. P Pryor, to be returned.

Professor Dwight having represented that Frederick P. Prior had died within a week after entering the Law School, it was ordered that the fee be returned to his father, Mr. Roger A. Pryor.

1873, April 7.
Fee refunded to J. Constable.

Resolved, That the Treasurer be authorized to refund to James Constable, admitted to the School of Mines February 4, 1873, but who has never been able to attend the exercises of the School, the amount of his tuition fee, one hundred dollars, paid in advance for the current term.

1873, May 5.
Mr. Aymar's fee for Drawing to be refunded.

Resolved, That the Treasurer be authorized to refund to Mr. José Aymar, of the Senior Class, the amount of the fee paid by him for instruction in drawing in the School of Mines, and that no fee be hereafter exacted from students in the Academic Department to whom such privilege may be accorded.

FELLOWSHIPS.

1872, Oct. 2.
Fellowships.

Whereas, It is not consistent with the intention of this Board, in the establishment of fellowships to be holden by graduates of the college, that the holder of any such fellowship shall, while in the enjoyment of the same, engage in business pursuits or in studies not in harmony with the subjects of his fellowship, therefore *Resolved*, That in case the holder of any fellowship in the gift of the college shall so engage in business during the term of his fellowship, or fail to devote himself faithfully to the studies, which, by the terms of the resolution establishing such fellowship, he is required to pursue, he shall forfeit the benefit attached to the same by the terms of said resolution.

<small>1873, Mar. 3.
Fellows not to engage in business.</small> *Resolved*, That in case any student or graduate, who shall have been admitted to a Fellowship in the gift of the Trustees of this College, shall, at any time during the term to which such appointment extends, engage in the affairs of business, or in any professional studies not, in the opinion of the President, in harmony with subjects of his Fellowship, he shall, from that time forward, cease to be entitled to the benefits of such Fellowship.

<small>1873, April 7.
Fellows may attend lectures without charge.</small> *Resolved*, That it be permitted to any person holding a Fellowship in Letters or Science in the gift of this Board, to attend any of the regular exercises of the College or of the School of Mines in departments of study which are in harmony with the subject of his said Fellowship, without any charge for tuition; provided that his object in so attending be to fit himself for a life of literary labor or scientific research, and not to prepare for the practice of any profession

<small>1873, April 7.
Fellowships.</small> The resolution in relation to Fellowships, passed at the last meeting, was reconsidered, and amended by inserting the words "in the opinion of the President," before "in harmony with."

FINANCIAL POLICY, PERMANENT.

<small>1870, May 2.
Unexpended balances.</small> *Resolved*, That any balances which may remain unexpended at the close of the present financial year, of appropriations to the purposes hereinafter named, viz.: to the Library of the College for the Departments of Physics, of Mechanics, &c., and of Chemistry, to the Botanical Library and Herbarium, and to the furnishing of the

President's House; also, to the Library of the School of Mines, to the departments of Analytical Chemistry, of Mineralogy, Metallurgy, and the Metallurgical Laboratory, of Geology and Paleontology, and of Civil and Mining Engineering and Drawing, be carried forward and added to the appropriations for the same objects which may be made for the ensuing financial year.

GEBHARD FUND.

1868, Dec. 7.
Gebhard Prof.

Resolved, That the Treasurer be authorized to pay to the Gebhard Professor, the excess of the income of the Gebhard fund for the last financial year, over the salary allowed to the Professor for the same period, being $260.70.

1869, Nov. 1.
Payment to the Gebhard Professor.

Resolved, That the Treasurer be authorized to pay to the Gebhard Professor two hundred and forty-three dollars and thirty-eight cents, being the excess of the income of the Gebhard Fund for the financial year last past, over the salary allowed to the professor for the same period.

1870, Nov. 7.
Gebhard Professor.

Ordered, That the Treasurer be authorized to pay to the Gebhard Professor one hundred and thirty-six dollars and thirteen cents, being the difference between the income of the Gebhard fund for the last preceding financial year, and the salary allowed to the Professor for the same period.

1871, Nov. 6.
Interest on Gebhard Fund.

Likewise *Resolved*, That interest at the rate of seven per cent. per annum, from the first day of July last, be paid on the Gebhard Fund.

1873, Nov. 3.
$298 03 to be paid to Prof. Schmidt.

Resolved, That the Treasurer be authorized to pay to the Gebhard Professor two hundred and ninety-eight dollars and three cents, for the difference between the income of the Gebhard Fund for the financial year and the amount allowed to him for salary for the same period.

HERBARIUM.

1870, June 6.
Appropriation Herbarium.

Resolved, That a sum not exceeding two hundred dollars be appropriated to be expended by Dr. Torrey in employing a competent assistant to aid him in bringing up the large arrears of labor in the Herbarium, occasioned by the very large additions to the collection which have been received during the past year.

1871, Oct. 2.
Appropriation for rooms for Herbarium, &c.

Resolved, That a sum not exceeding seventy dollars be appropriated to be expended under the direction of Dr. Torrey, for the purchase or repair of furniture for the apartments in the College occupied by the Herbarium and Botanic Library.

1871, Dec. 4.
Thanks to Mr. J. J. Crooke.

Resolved, That the thanks of the Trustees be presented to J. J. Crooke, Esq., for his liberal proposition to purchase and present to the Herbarium of the college a portion of the valuable Herbarium of Prof. Neisner of Berne, at a cost of two thousand five hundred dollars; and also for his contributions heretofore made in aid of the botanical collection.

1873, Jan. 6.
$200 appropriated for shelves for Meissner Botanical Collection.

Resolved, That a sum not exceeding two hundred dollars be appropriated for the construction of suitable shelves and wall cases for the reception of the Meissner botanical collection recently presented to the college by J. J. Crooke, Esq.

1873, April 7.
Custodian of the Herbarium.

Resolved, That the President be authorized to engage the services of some competent person to take charge and have the care of the Herbarium and Botanical Library of the college, at a compensation not to exceed one thousand dollars per annum.

INSTRUCTION, COMMITTEE ON COURSE OF.

1868, Oct. 5.
Conservation of Force and Connection of Science transferred.
Resolved, That the subjects, "Conservation of Force" and "Connection of the Sciences," be transferred from the programme of lectures of the *second* year, in the School of Mines, to that of lectures of the third year.

Quanti'tive Blowpipe.
Resolved, further, that the subject of "Quantitative Blowpipe Analysis" be dropped from the programme of the course of the third year.

1869, April 5.
Civil Engineering.
Resolved, That it be referred to the Committee on the School of Mines to inquire into the expediency of creating a Chair of Civil Engineering and a Chair of Modern Languages in said school.

1869, May 3.
Civil Engineering.
Resolved, That it be referred to the Board of Trustees to make provision for giving hereafter, in the School of Mines, a full and satisfactory course of instruction in civil engineering.

1869, May 3.
French and German.
Resolved, That it be recommended to the Board of Trustees to make provision for the employment of a competent instructor in the French and German languages; and that the president be authorized to employ some suitable person to give such instruction in the School of Mines, to hold his position during the pleasure of the trustees.

Resolved, That the foregoing recommendations be made upon the understanding that the pecuniary situation of the college will justify incurring the expense.

Resolved, That the above resolutions be referred back to the committee to consider further and report.

1869, Oct. 4.
Civil Engineeri'g.
On his motion (treasurer's), *Resolved,* That the part of the president's report, relating to a chair of civil engineering

in the School of Mines, be referred to the committee on that school to consider and report.

1869, Oct 4.
Instruction in the Evidences.

Resolved, That the committee on the course be instructed to report as to the best mode of providing for instruction in the Evidences of Religion.

1869, Dec. 6.
French and German.

Resolved, That it be referred to the Committee on the School of Mines to consider and report to this Board at the meeting in January next, what permanent provision ought to be made for the instruction of the students of the School of Mines in French and German.

1869, Dec. 6.
Civil Engin'ring

Resolved, That civil engineering be taught in the School of Mines; that the instruction in that subject be committed to the Professor of Mining Engineering; and that the title of the Professor hereafter shall be, "Professor of Civil and Mining Engineering."

1870, Jan. 3.
Instruction in French and German in the School of Mines.

Mr. Betts, from the Committee of the School of Mines, reported that the committee had agreed to report to the Board that it was expedient that regular instruction in German and French should be given in the School of Mines; and that arrangements should be made for appointing and employing regular instructors in those languages; such instruction to begin at the commencement of the academic year in October next; and that in the mean time the necessary details should be prepared by the Committee of the School of Mines; and that said committee be authorized in their discretion to confer with the faculty of the School of Mines; whereupon it was

Resolved, That the recommendation of the Committee be adopted.

Resolved, That the expense attending the same shall not exceed the annual sum of $2,000.

1870, May 2.
Special course.

Resolved, That the Board of the College be requested to report to the Trustees at their next meeting whether in their opinion it would be advantageous or otherwise to admit students who are not candidates for a degree in Arts to attend the exercises of the College in some of its departments without taking the full course, and in case of an affirmative answer, to suggest the conditions or limitations according to which this privilege should be regulated.

1870, May 2.
Instructors in French and German.

Resolved, That the Committee on the School of Mines be authorized to recommend some properly qualified person to give instruction in the French language to the students of the School of Mines, the said instructor being expected to enter upon his duties on the first Monday in October next; to give, if required, eight lessons per week to classes in said School throughout the scholastic year; and to receive compensation at the rate of one thousand dollars a year for such service.

Resolved, further, That if the Board of Trustees shall see fit to authorize or require instruction in French to be given to undergraduate students, then the same instructor may be employed to give, if required, four lessons per week throughout the scholastic year, to undergraduate classes, regular or voluntary, and that in case the amount of service rendered by him be so increased, his compensation shall be also increased to twelve hundred dollars per annum.

Resolved, further, That the Committee have power to recommend some other suitably qualified person to give instruction in the German language, such instructor to enter upon his duties on the first Monday in October next, and to be compensated at the rate of one thousand dollars per annum.

1870, June 6.
Evidences.
Rev. W. A. McVickar.

Resolved, That the Rev. W. A. McVickar, be requested to give instruction to the Senior Class during the ensuing year, in the Evidences of Natural and Revealed Religion and that it be referred to the Standing Committee to fix the compensation.

INSTRUCTION, COMMITTEE ON COURSE OF.

1870, Nov. 7.
Committee on Course to report on engagement of Prof. Raymond

Resolved, That it be referred to the Committee on the Course, to consider the proposition of Prof. R. R. Raymond to give instruction to the undergraduates in the College in practical elocution, and to inquire and report on the expediency of engaging the services of Prof. Raymond for that purpose; and in case of an affirmative conclusion, to report on what terms and conditions such an engagement ought to be made.

1871, Oct. 2.
Referred to Committee in relation to assistants to professors.

Resolved, That it be referred to the Committee on the Course to inquire whether the interest of the College would be, to any important degree, promoted by the appointment of an officer, or officers, of a higher degree than tutor, in aid of any of the existing Professorships, and that said committee present their report at the next stated meeting of this Board.

1871, Nov. 6.
Chairman Committee on Course.

Resolved, That the Committee on the Course have power to appoint their own chairman.

1872, March 2.

Resolved, That it is inexpedient to appoint another assistant in the Department of Mineralogy and Metallurgy.

Resolved, That it shall be the duty of the Faculty of the School of Mines, as soon as practicable, to prescribe to the students, both regular and special, certain hours of attendance for practice in the laboratories of the Departments of Analytical Chemistry, and of Metallurgy, and in Drawing; and that the attendance of the students for practice in each of such departments of instruction shall be confined to the hours so prescribed.

1872, April 1.
Assistant in Mineralogy and Metallurgy.

Resolved, That it is inexpedient to appoint another assistant in the department of Mineralogy and Metallurgy.

Attendance for practice in Chemistry.

Resolved, That it shall be the duty of the Faculty of the School of Mines as soon as practicable to prescribe to the students, both regular and special, certain hours of attendance for practice in the laboratories of the departments of Analytical Chemistry, and of Metallurgy, and in Drawing; and that the attendance of the students for practice in each of such departments of instruction shall be confined to the hours so prescribed.

<small>1873, March 3. Instruction in chemistry referred to the Committee on School of Mines.</small> *Resolved,* That it be referred to the Committee on the School of Mines to inquire and report whether arrangements cannot be made to secure greater fulness and thoroughness in the instruction of the students of the school in General Chemistry; and that they report to the Board on the subjects at the next stated meeting.

<small>1873, April 7. Report and Resolution of Committee on School of Mines.</small> *Resolved,* That the Professor of General Chemistry in the college be required to give a course of instruction to the preparatory class in the School of Mines, in conformity with the scheme prescribed by this Board by resolution of May 4, 1868, of three hours per week throughout the year, completing the subject of Inorganic Chemistry in the first session of the college year, and the subject of Organic Chemistry in the second session; and that the instruction be given to that class alone, and not in combination with any class in chemistry belonging to the college, and be conducted with special reference to the wants of students preparing themselves to engage in scientific professions.

Resolved, That the Professor of Analytical and Applied Chemistry be required to give a course of higher instruction, of three hours per week throughout the year, in General Chemistry, with special attention to theory, to the class of the First Year in the School of Mines, in completing the course of Inorganic Chemistry during the first session and the course of Organic Chemistry during the second; and that, in consideration of this addition to his labors, he be relieved of the duty of giving instruction in Qualitative and Quantitative Analysis, but continue personally to instruct in Stoichiometry and in Applied Chemistry, as heretofore.

Resolved, further, That the offices of assistant in Qualitative Analysis and assistant in Quantitative Analysis be discontinued after the close of the present year, and that in place of them there be and are hereby created, the offices of instructor in Qualitative and instructor in Quantitative Analysis, to be charged under the direction of the Professor of Analytical and Applied Chemistry, with the duties heretofore performed by the said assistants respectively, and with the further duty of giving instruction, two hours per week each throughout the year, in the theory of Analytical Chemistry in their aforesaid respective departments; and that such instructors be compensated for their services at the rate of fifteen hundred dollars per annum. Laid over.

1873, June 3.
Assistant in Mathematics, School of Mines.

Resolved, That the President be authorized to engage the services of some competent person, a graduate, if possible, of the college or of the School of Mines, to serve as assistant in Mathematics in said school, with the compensation of one thousand dollars per annum, payable in instalments, in like manner as the other assistants in the school are paid; and that the name of the person so engaged be reported to the Trustees for confirmation at their stated meeting in October next.

1873, Oct. 6.
Assistant in Mathematics in the School of Mines.

Resolved, That there be appointed an assistant in the department of Pure Mathematics in the School of Mines, to be compensated at the same rate and in the same manner as the other assistants now employed in said school, viz., one thousand dollars per annum payable in six equal instalments, at dates heretofore fixed for such assistants by resolution of the Trustees.

LIBRARY, COMMITTEE ON THE.

1871, April 3.

Resolved, That the Committee on the Library shall hereafter consist of four members, elected from the Board of Trustees, together with the President of the College, who shall be a member "ex-officio."

MISCELLANEOUS.

1871, Oct. 2.
Union of libraries of College and School of Mines.

Resolved, That so much of the President's Report as relates to the expediency of uniting the Library of the School of Mines with that of the College, and to a desired provision of a place in the College buildings, in which students may prepare their college exercises when not in attendance with their classes, be referred to the Library Committee and the Committee on the School of Mines, to consider and report whether such a union of the libraries is expedient, and if so, what measures should be adopted for their preservation, government, and use, and whether accommodation could be provided in the Library for the use of unoccupied students, and if so, what arrangements would be necessary for that purpose.

1872, April 1.
Report of Joint Committee of Library and School of Mines on Library, &c.

1*st*. That it is inexpedient at the present time to enter upon the subject of the union of the two libraries.

2*d*. That it is not possible to provide accommodations in the Library for unoccupted students.

3*d*. That the only building which, in their judgment, can be used for that purpose is the one now occupied by Professor Joy and Dr. Torrey; but as the Committee have no authority to propose any alterations in the building, they prefer that the subject be left in the hands of the Trustees.

The report was approved.

MISCELLANEOUS.

1871, Dec. 4.
Overflow from Prof.Joy's laboratory.

Resolved, That any professor from whose laboratory or apartment an overflow of water shall hereafter occur, will be held personally responsible for any damage occasioned thereby.

PRESIDENT, OF THE.

1869, Oct. 4.
President relieved from instruction.

Resolved, That the President be relieved from the duty of instruction in the college.

OBSERVATORY, ASTRONOMICAL.

1872, Feb. 5th.
Appropriation of $1,500 for telescope.

The resolution passed at the last meeting making an appropriation of fifteen hundred dollars for the purchase of a portable telescope and spectroscope was, under the permanent financial ordinance, again considered and passed.

1872, Nov. 4.
Building for the telescope.

Resolved, That the Professor of Mechanics and Astronomy be authorized to apply, with the approval of the President, under the supervision of the Standing Committee, such portion of the balance remaining unexpended of the appropriations heretofore annually made for the benefit of his department, as may be necessary to provide a suitable structure on the college ground, for the protection and convenient use of the telescope ordered for the college, under resolution of the Trustees, February 5, 1872.

1873, March 3.
Assistant in the Observatory.

Resolved, That an assistant be appointed to the Professor of Mathematics and Astronomy in the Observatory at a compensation of six hundred dollars per annum, with the privilege of occupying a room in the college buildings; payment to be made in six equal instalments at the same times at which the assistants in the School of Mines are paid.

Mr. L Waldo appointed.

Resolved, That Mr. Leonard Waldo be appointed assistant to the Professor of Astronomy for the Observatory, his term of service to date from January 1, 1873, entitling him to the payment of the instalments of salary for the current academic year.

METEOROLOGICAL OBSERVATIONS—PRINTING. 41

1873, March 3.
$100 appropriated to furnish his room.

Resolved, That a sum not exceeding one hundred dollars be appropriated to purchase suitable furniture for a room in the college, to be occupied by the assistant to the Professor of Mathematics and Astronomy, the same to be expended under the direction of the President.

1873, Dec. 1.
$1,000 appropriated to Mr. Waldo.

Resolved, That, in order to enable Mr. Waldo, the Assistant in Astronomy, to accompany one of the expeditions to be sent out by the United States to observe the Transit of Venus in 1874, $1,000, in addition to his salary, be appropriated to his use during his absence, the amount to be paid as may be agreed upon with the Treasurer.

METEOROLOGICAL OBSERVATIONS.

1870, April 4.
Meteorological observations discontinued.

Resolved, That the meteorological observations in the College be discontinued.

PRINTING.

1868, June 1.
Thanks to Dr. Drisler.

Resolved, That the thanks of this Board be presented to Dr. Drisler for his able and deeply interesting address, commemorative of the life and services of Dr. Anthon, and that a copy of the address be requested for publication.

Copies of Dr. Drisler's address.

Resolved, That in case this request be complied with, the President be authorized to cause an impression of five hundred copies to be printed for distribution.

1869, May 3.
Laws, etc., affecting College.

Resolved, That a new edition of the charters and laws of the State affecting the college be published under the direction of a committee consisting of two trustees.

The clerk and the treasurer were appointed the committee.

1870, Dec. 19. New edition Statutes to be printed.	*Resolved*, That a new edition of the Statutes shall be printed under the direction of the President, to which shall be prefixed the Historical Sketch.
1871, Oct. 2. Paper on "Metric System" to be printed.	A paper by the President, on the "Metric System," which had been read before the "University Convocation," having been presented, it was ordered that a thousand copies be printed at the expense of the Board.
1872, June 3. General Catalogue.	*Resolved*, That the General Catalogue of the Trustees, Officers, Alumni, and honorary graduates of the college be hereafter, and until the further order of this Board, published only at the end of each alternate triennium; and that the next publication of the same be not made until after the end of the academic year 1876–77.

PRIZE SCHOLARSHIPS AND PRIZES.

1868, June 1. Examining Committee on the Greek Prizes.	*Resolved*, That the regulations for the examination for the prizes in Greek, lately established, be so modified as to admit that the examining committee may be made up of those members to be selected by the president from the Alumni not connected with the college, and from the professors in the classical department in the college, as may be most convenient.
1871, April 3. Scholarships and fellowships.	*Resolved*, That the plan reported by the Committee on the Statutes, providing for the establishment of Scholarships and Fellowships in the college, be adopted; and that the Board of the College be requested to make the necessary announcements and arrangements for carrying the same into effect; so that the first competitive examination for said Scholarships and Fellowships may be held immediately after the final examination of the classes in June, 1872.

PRIZE SCHOLARSHIPS AND PRIZES.

Payments of scholarships and fellowships. *Resolved,* That the payments which may become due in each Academic Year on account of the Scholarships and Fellowships provided for as above, shall be made in two equal instalments, payable on the 15th November and May in each year.

1872, Dec. 2. *Resolved,* That the modifications in the scheme of Prize Scholarships, recommended to the Trustees in the resolution of the Board of the College, adopted October 25, 1872, and read to-day [Nov. 4], before the Trustees in the minutes of said Board [the same being in the words following, viz.: *Resolved,* That the Board of the College respectfully recommend to the Board of Trustees to so modify the present scheme of scholarships that there shall be established one scholarship for each of the principal branches of study in each of three lower classes viz.: in the Freshman Class one each in Greek, Latin, Mathematics, and Rhetoric, with English composition; in the Sophomore Class one each in Greek, Latin, Mathematics, and History; in the Junior Class one each in Greek, Latin, Mechanics, Chemistry, Physics, and Logic, with English Literature—the examinations for such scholarships in each class to be on the regular class studies of the year, with such additional matter (if deemed advisable) as may be determined before hand by the President and the Professors in the respective departments] be, and the same are hereby approved and adopted to take effect at the next and all subsequent examinations for scholarships until otherwise ordered.

1873, June 2. Prizes in English. *Resolved,* That two prizes in Rhetoric and English Composition of $100 and $50 be established, to be competed for by written examinations and theses at the end of the Senior year; and that it be referred to the Board of the College to report suitable regulations.

1873, Dec. 1. Prizes in English amended. *Resolved,* That the resolution of this Board establishing prizes to be competed for in the Department of English, by members of the Senior Class, be amended by striking from the clause, "to be competed for by written examinations and theses," the words "examinations and," so that said clause, as amended, may read, "to be competed for by written theses."

PROFESSORSHIPS AND PROFESSORS.

1868, Dec. 7. Resolution on Dr. McVickar's death.

Whereas, The Rev. John McVickar, S. T. D., Emeritus Professor of the Evidences of Natural and Revealed Religion, in Columbia College, has, since the last meeting of the trustees, been called to his final rest, the Board of Trustees of Columbia College place on record the following minute expressive of their respect for the deceased, and their appreciation of the services rendered by him to the college during the long course of years in which he was connected with this institution.

The memory of Dr. McVickar must always be cherished with deep and peculiar interest, as that of one who was eminent for high attainments, finished scholarship and varied and extensive learning, and a sincere and unaffected religious character. His labors were rewarded by their acknowledged results in the characters which he had aided in forming; to him society was indebted for strong influences exerted in the cause of Christian morals and of humane letters from the conspicuous chair which he so ably filled; and evidences of the personal attachment of his pupils and the high respect entertained for him throughout this community constituted a tribute grateful to his declining years.

This Board, while they submit to that inevitable decree, in pursuance of which the wise and venerable fathers of our race are ever passing away, do so with regret at the shortness of the time during which their acquisitions, at the highest point of completeness, are available; and they unite with other bodies directly interested in the present sad event in expressing their sorrow at its occurrence, and their affectionate recollection of the reverend and venerable deceased :

Resolved, That a copy of these resolutions be transmitted to the family of the Rev. Dr. McVickar.

1869, March 1.
Leave of absence Prof. Schmidt.

Resolved, That leave of absence be granted to Professor Schmidt, for the remainder of the present academic year, provided his health should not so far improve, in the meantime, as to enable him with prudence to resume his duties in the college.

Resolved, That the President be authorized, should it appear to be necessary, to employ, at the same rate of compensation now allowed to other tutors, some suitable person to discharge such duties as in consequence of the absence of Professor Schmidt cannot be otherwise properly performed until such time as Professor Schmidt shall resume his classes, or until this Board shall otherwise order ; but such employment shall not extend beyond the present academic term.

1870, June 3.
Prof. Nairne's leave of absence.

Resolved, That the leave of absence heretofore granted to Professor Nairne, to expire at the close of the present session, be extended to the end of the academic year ; and that the President be authorized to engage the services of Mr. Knox to discharge the duties of Professor Nairne's department during the ensuing session on the same terms as heretofore, to wit, for the sum of one thousand dollars as the compensation for said entire session.

1870, Feb. 7.
Resolution on Fench and German laid on the table and afterwards passed.

Resolved, That the President be authorized to employ a teacher or teachers to give instruction in the French and German languages in the School of Mines during the second session of the current academic year, provided that the services of a competent person can be secured for that object at an expense not exceeding five hundred dollars.

PROFESSORSHIPS AND PROFESSORS.

1870, Feb. 7.
Evidences.

Resolved, That the President be authorized to engage some competent person to give instruction in the Evidences of Revealed Religion during the *remainder* of the present collegiate year, for a compensation not exceeding five hundred dollars.

1870, April 4.
Professor of French and German.

Resolved, That this Board will, on the first Monday of May next, proceed to elect a Professor of the French and German Languages, the said Professor being expected to enter upon his duties on the first Monday in October next; to give, if required, eight lessons per week in each language to classes in the School of Mines throughout the scholastic year, and to receive compensation at the rate of two thousand dollars a year for such service.

Salary $2,000.

To teach in College if required.

Resolved further, That if the Board of Trustees shall see fit to authorize or require instruction in French to be given to undergraduate students, then the same Professor may be employed to give four lessons per week throughout the scholastic year to undergraduate classes, regular or voluntary, and that in case the amount of service rendered by him be so increased his compensation shall be also increased to two thousand two hundred dollars per annum.

Salary $200 additional.

1870, June 6.
Title of Professor of Mechanics.

A Resolution, That the title of the Professor of Mechanics in the School of Mines be changed so that it may hereafter read Professor of Mechanics, Practical Astronomy and Geodesy, was referred to the Committee on the Course to consider and report.

1871, Oct. 2.
Resolution about instruction in French, Professor Loiseau.

Resolved, That the President be authorized to assign to Professor Loiseau, a room in the College or School of Mines, in which to receive classes in French after the close of the exercises of the College or School of Mines for the day, provided this can be done without interfering with the operations of either department or incommoding any of the officers; and provided also, that Professor Loiseau shall consent to receive into such classes, students of the college, or the school, on such terms as shall be approved by the President and the Treasurer.

PROFESSORSHIPS AND PROFESSORS. 47

Prof. De Ternos, the same. *Resolved*, That the President be authorized to extend the same privilege to Professor De Ternos, for receiving classes in Spanish, subject to the same conditions.

1871, Dec. 1. Leave of absence to Prof. Newberry. On like motion, *Resolved*, That leave of absence be granted to Professor Newberry, for the remainder of the term.

Lecture by Prof. B. W Hawkins. On like motion, *Resolved*, That Professor B. Waterhouse Hawkins be engaged to deliver two lectures per week to the classes of the first year in the School of Mines in Zoology; two lectures per week to the class of the second year in General Geology; and two lectures per week to the class of the third year in Paleontology, for the three weeks, commencing December 4, 1871, at a compensation of one hundred per week for the said six lectures, or three hundred dollars for the entire time of said engagement.

1871, Dec. 4. Leave of absence to Prof. Drisler. *Resolved*, That leave of absence be given to Professor Drisler until the close of the Christmas holidays, or for such longer time as his medical adviser may deem necessary.

Instruction in his absence. *Resolved*, That the Board of the College be requested to make such arrangements, if possible, as to provide instruction for Professor Drisler's class during his absence.

1872, Feb. 5. Adjunct Professor of Literature, &c. *Resolved*, That there be and there hereby is established in the department of Philosophy and English Literature an Adjunct Professorship, the Professor holding the same to give instruction in History and Rhetoric, and to discharge such other duties as may be assigned to him by the Professor, with the approval of the President and of the Board of Trustees; said Adjunct Professor to be compensated at the rate of two thousand dollars per annum.

Resolved, That an election be held to fill the chair of Adjunct Professor of Philosophy and English Literature created by the foregoing resolution, on the first Monday in May, 1872; and that the term of office of said Adjunct Professor shall commence at the commencement of the next academic session, viz., October 1st, 1872, from which date he shall be entitled to receive compensation as above provided; to hold his office during the pleasure of this Board.

1872, March 2. *Resolved,* That the consideration of the expediency of the purchase of apparatus applied for by Professor Egleston be deferred until the appropriations of the next succeeding year shall be made.

A communication was received from Professor Egleston, asking to be relieved from his lectures until the fifteenth of February next; upon which it was

1872, Dec. 2.
Leave of absence to Prof. Egleston.
Resolved, That the request of Prof. Egleston be granted, and that the President be authorized to employ Mr. H. B. Cornwall, and Mr. John A. Church, or such other competent person or persons as he may select, to discharge the duties of Prof. Egleston, until the end of the present session of the School of Mines, February 15, at such rates of compensation as may be agreed upon, with the approval of the Standing Committee.

1873, Jan. 6.
Committee to confer with Prof. Egleston.
Resolved, That the communication of Professor Egleston on the subject of his health be referred to a Special Committee of two to confer with him touching the same, with the view of ascertaining at what future time he feels confident of being able to resume his duties in School of Mines; for the purpose of enabling this Board to judge as to the most suitable mode of providing for the instruction of his classes during the interval.

1873, Feb. 3.
Prof. Egleston.
Resolved, That a further leave of absence be granted to Professor Egleston, from the twelfth of February to the first of October next, and that the President be, and is hereby authorized to employ proper assistants to discharge the duties of the Professorship in the interim, with the express proviso, however, that the extra expenses

incurred in maintaining his department be borne by the Professor, and deducted from his salary.

<small>1873, March 3.
Leave of absence to Professor Egleston.</small> *Resolved,* That a further leave of absence be granted to Professor Egleston, from the twelfth of February to the 1st of October next, and the President be and is hereby authorized to employ proper assistants to discharge the duties of the Professorship in the interim; with the express proviso, however, that the extra expenses incurred in maintaining his department be borne by the Professor, and deducted from his salary.

<small>1873, June 3.
Prof Van Amringe.</small> *Resolved,* That the word "adjunct" be stricken from the title of Professor Van Amringe, and that his title hereafter be "Professor of Mathematics."

<small>1873, Oct. 6.
Leave of absence to Prof. Egleston.</small> *Resolved,* That the leave of absence of Prof. Egleston be extended till the 15th day of February next, upon the same conditions as those specified in the resolution of the 3d of March last, by which his leave was extended to October 1, 1873.

<small>His duties to be provided for.</small> *Resolved,* That the President be authorized to engage some suitable person or persons to give instruction in the subjects belonging to Prof. Egleston's department during the session now beginning, and that the Treasurer be authorized to pay to such person or persons as compensation for such services an amount not exceeding two hundred dollars per month for metallurgy, and two hundred dollars per month for mineralogy and blow-pipe analysis.

REPAIRS.

1868, June 1.
Alterations in College buildings.
Resolved, That the Treasurer and President be empowered to make such alterations in the college buildings as they may deem expedient, at a cost not exceeding five hundred dollars.

ESTIMATED FOR REPAIRS, &c.

1869, May 3.
Repairs.

Flagging Fourth avenue	$200	
" Forty-ninth street	50	
		$250
Area School of Mines Fiftieth street	$200	
Sewer connections	125	
		325
Ceiling Qualitative Laboratory	$110	
		110
Painting and whitewashing School of Mines	$200–300	
Similar purposes for the College		150

1870, June 6.
Repairs, President's house.
Resolved, That it be referred to a Committee of the Board to inquire and report at the regular meeting in October next, whether any and, if any, what repairs and improvements are required in and about the President's house, and to what extent such repairs, &c., if necessary, ought to be chargeable to the College.

1871, June 5.
Repairs to College and President's house.
Resolved, That the Standing Committee have authority to direct such repairs to the exterior of the college building as shall appear to be necessary; and also to the cesspool in the rear of the President's house, and to the flagging and steps of the same houses, at a cost, for the whole, not to exceed one thousand five hundred dollars.

Resolved, That it be referred to the Standing Committee to cause to be done to the exterior wood-work and blinds of the President's house such painting as they shall deem to be expedient.

1871, Oct. 2.
Bill for Professor Peck's room be paid.
Ordered, That a bill of George G. Gregory, of one hundred and two dollars and fifteen cents, for alterations in Professor Peck's room, be paid.

1872, June 3.
$300 for repairs.

Resolved, That a sum of not exceeding three hundred dollars be appropriated for the purpose of defraying the expense of repairs which may be necessary about the building and in the house of the Janitor; provided, in the latter case such repairs shall, in the judgment of the President, be properly chargeable to the college; and also to renewing the fixtures, furniture, or paint, in such class-rooms as may require such renewals; the same to be expended under the direction of the President.

ROWING.

1872, June 3.
Resolution about Boat Club referred to Standing Committee.

Resolved, That the petition of the Committee of the Class of 1875, asking for aid from the Trustees in the establishing of an association for boating in the Harlem River, and for defraying the expenses of boats, oars, and boat-houses, and for rent for a site for the same, be referred to the Standing Committee, with instructions to report at the stated meeting of the Trustees in October next.

1872, Nov. 4.
Rowing.

Resolved, That any appropriations that may hereafter be made for the encouragement of the exercise of rowing among the students of the undergraduate course, shall be subject to the following regulations:

First. All applications of the fund shall be made under the direction of a committee of five, to be composed of a Professor, to be appointed by the Board of the College, who shall be chairman of the committee, and a member from each class, who shall be appointed annually by a majority of his classmates.

Second. Such committee shall have charge of all property purchased or hired by means of the appropriation hereby made, and shall enact such rules and regulations as they shall think proper, in regard to the conditions on which students shall enjoy the benefit of the provision made by these resolutions, and their conduct when engaged in such exercises.

Third. Such students, and such only as shall subscribe a declaration that they will observe and obey all rules and regulations made, or that shall be made, by such committee, shall be entitled to the advantage of the provisions hereby made.

Fourth. The assent of the Chairman shall be requisite to give validity to any act of the committee.

Fifth. No payment on account of such appropriation shall be made, except on presentation to the Treasurer, of bills therefor certified by such Chairman and by the President.

$1,000 appropriated.

Resolved, That one thousand dollars be appropriated for the present year for the encouragement of the exercise of rowing among the students of the undergraduate course.

SALARIES.

1868, Nov. 2.
Mr. Rennell.

Resolved, That the treasurer be authorized to pay to Mr. Frederic Rennell forty dollars, as a compensation for clerical services tendered by him during the sickness of the president's secretary.

1868, Dec. 7.
Executors of Dr. McVickar.

Resolved, That the treasurer be authorized to pay to the executors of the Rev John McVickar, D.D., deceased, his salary as emeritus professor up to the 15th day of November last.

1868, Dec. 7.
Increase of salaries.

Resolved, That the provisions of the resolution of January 6, 1868, granting a temporary increase of salary and compensation of fifty per cent. upon the salaries as established by resolution of this board, February 5, 1866, to the president and professors and the other officers therein specified, be continued in force for one year from the 15th of November, 1868, and that the benefit of this resolution be made applicable also to Professor Short and to the librarian.

SALARIES.

1868, Dec. 7.
Increase of salaries S. of M.
Resolved, That the provisions of the same date, January 6, 1868, granting a temporary increase of twenty-five per cent. in the salaries, as therein specified, of the professors of the School of Mines, be likewise continued in force for one year from the 15th day of November, 1868.

1868, Dec. 7.
A. C. Merriam. Salary.
Resolved, That the treasurer be authorized to pay to Mr. A. C. Merriam, tutor in Latin and Greek, as compensation for his services for the time elapsing between October 1 and November 15, 1868, the same amount to which his predecessor, Mr. Everson, would have been entitled for that period, if he had continued to hold the office.

1868, Dec. 7.
Weeks' allowance.
Resolved, That the allowance to Mr. Weeks, janitor, of two hundred dollars per annum, in addition to his salary, and the temporary allowance this day made, be extended to the academic year ending September 30, 1869, and made payable in the same intervals as heretofore.

1868, Dec. 7.
Prof. Van Amringe's salary.
Resolved, That the salary of Professor Van Amringe be increased to $4,000, and that he be allowed the same additional sum granted this day to the other professors.

1869, Feb. 1.
Prof. Van Amringe's salary.
Resolved, That the increase of the salary of Professor Van Amringe take effect from the 15th of November, 1868.

1869, Oct. 4.
Salaries.
Resolved, That the subject of the salaries of the officers of the college and board be referred to a special committee to consist of five members.

Mr. Nash, the Rev. Dr. Hutton, Mr. Jones, Mr. Rutherford, and Judge Blatchford were appointed the committee.

1869, Nov. 1.
Weeks' compensation.
Resolved, That the sum of two hundred dollars be granted to the janitor of the college, Mr. S. R. Weeks, in addition to his compensation, otherwise provided, for the current financial year, the same to be paid in equal quarterly instalments, at the usual time of paying salaries.

SALARIES.

1869, Dec. 6.
Payment to Prof. Lamoroux.

Resolved, That the Treasurer be authorized to pay to Prof. Wendell Lamoroux the sum of one hundred and fifty dollars, being the amount by which the sum paid him as compensation for his services during the academic year 1868–9 falls short of the annual compensation paid for a similar amount of service to other officers of the same grade.

1869, Dec. 20.
Increase of salaries.

Resolved, That the provisions of the resolution of January 6, 1868, granting a temporary increase of salary and compensation of fifty per cent. upon the salaries of the President, professors and the other officers and persons therein named, be continued in force for one year from the 15th of November, 1869, and that the benefits of this resolution be made applicable to Professor Short and to the Librarian.

Resolved, That the provisions of the resolution of January 6, 1868, granting a temporary increase of twenty-five per cent. on the salaries of the Professors of the School of Mines, be likewise continued in force for one year from the 15th of November, 1869.

Resolved, That the salary of the Treasurer be $4,000 from the 15th of November, 1869, together with the temporary increase for one year from said date of fifty per cent. made to the salary of the Treasurer by the said resolution of January 6, 1868.

1870, March 7.
Salaries in School of Mines referred.

Resolved, That it be referred to a special committee to consider whether there exists any just reason for increasing the compensation of any of the assistants employed in the Scientific departments of the College or School of Mines, with power to recommend such increase if they find that impartial justice requires any such claim to be admitted.

1870, April 4.
Salaries of Assistants in Geology and Mineralogy raised.

Resolved, That the salaries of the assistant of the Professor of Geology and Paleontology and of the assistant of the Professor of Mineralogy be raised from five hundred to one thousand dollars, such increase to take place from the beginning of the current year.

SALARIES. 55

1870, May 2.
Salaries of Assistants in School of Mines.

Resolved, That the order of the Board increasing the salaries of the assistants in the departments of Geology, &c., and of Mineralogy, &c., passed at the last meeting of the Trustees, which order in its terms applies to the "current year," be construed to intend the present financial year, commencing on the 1st of October, 1869.

1870, Nov. 7.
Janitor's salary increased this year.

Resolved, That there be allowed to the janitor of the college in addition to his compensation as otherwise provided, the sum of two hundred dollars for the present academic year, to be paid as heretofore in monthly instalments.

1870, Dec. 5.
Temporary increase of salaries, College.

Resolved, That the provisions of the resolution of this Board, of January 6th, 1868, granting a temporary increase of fifty per cent. upon the salaries of the officers therein named, be continued in force for one year from the 15th of November last past, and be applicable also, for that period, to Prof. Short and the Librarian; and that such increase for such year shall be computed upon the salaries as now established.

Temporary increase of salaries, School of Mines.

Resolved, That the provisions of the resolution of this Board, of January 6th, 1868, granting a temporary increase of twenty-five per cent. upon the salaries of the Professors of the School of Mines be also continued in force from the 15th day of November, 1870; and that such increase for such year shall be computed upon the salaries as now established.

1871, Nov. 6.
Compensation S. R. Weeks.

Resolved, That the sum of two hundred dollars be granted to Mr. S. R. Weeks, the Janitor of the college, in addition to his compensation otherwise provided, for the current financial year, the same to be payable in equal quarterly instalments at the usual time of paying salaries.

1871, Nov. 6.
Additional compensation to officers of college, &c.

Resolved, That the provisions of the resolutions of January 6th, 1868, granting a temporary increase of salary and compensation of fifty per cent. upon the salaries of the President, Professors, and other officers and persons therein named, to be computed upon the salaries as now established, be continued in force for one year from the 15th November, 1871; and that the benefit of this resolution be made applicable to Professor Short and the Librarian.

<small>Also School of Mines.</small>
Resolved, That the provisions of the resolution of January 6th, 1868, granting a temporary increase of twenty-five per cent. on the salaries of the Professors of the School of Mines, be likewise continued in force for one year from the 15th day of November, 1871.

<small>1872, Jan. 2. Prof. Joy's Assistant.</small>
Resolved, That the salary of Prof. Joy's assistant be increased to seven hundred and fifty dollars a year, to take effect from the fifteenth day of November last.

<small>1872, June 3. Salary of Tutors referred to Committee on Course.</small>
Resolved, That it be referred to the Committee on the Course to inquire as to the expediency of increasing the salary now paid to the tutors in ancient languages and in Rhetoric and History, in consideration of the tried capacity of the present officers, and the desirability of retaining their services permanently; and that the Committee report to the Trustees on this subject at the stated meeting to be held in October next.

<small>1872, June 3. Mr. Blossom's case referred to Standing Committee.</small>
The following resolution, "*Resolved,* That the Treasurer be authorized to pay to P. M. Blossom the amount of his salary as Assistant Assayer in the School of Mines, falling due June 1, 1872, it appearing that his temporary absence from his post was owing to serious illness, and that the duties devolving upon him were satisfactorily provided for by arrangement with his colleagues," was referred to the Standing Committee with power, with instructions to report a form of order to be adopted by this Board, touching the absence of Professors and Instructors.

<small>1872, Nov. 4. Professor Lieber's salary to be paid to November 15.</small>
Resolved, That the salary of Professor Lieber be continued to the fifteenth of November instant, and paid to his widow.

SALARIES. 57

1872, Nov. 4.
$200 to Mr. Weeks
Resolved, That the sum of two nundred dollars be allowed to the Janitor of the College, Mr. Weeks, in addition to his regular salary for the present financial year, the same to be paid at such times and in such instalments as provided for the payment of similar allowances heretofore.

1872. Nov. 4.
Temporary increase of salaries.
Resolved, That the provisions of the resolutions of January 6, 1868, granting a temporary increase of salary and compensation of fifty per cent. upon the salaries of the President, Professors, and other officers and persons therein named, to be computed upon the salaries as now established, be continued in force for one year, from the 15th of November, 1872, and that the benefits of this resolution be made applicable to Professor Short and the Librarian.

December 2.
Temporary increase of salaries
Resolved, That the provisions of the resolution of January 6th, 1868, granting a temporary increase of twenty-five per cent. on the salaries of Professors of the School of Mines, be likewise continued in force for one year from the 15th of November, 1872.

Increase of Tutors' salaries.
Resolved, That the salary of the present tutor in Greek and Latin, and of the present tutor in Rhetoric and History, be increased to one thousand dollars per annum, from the fifteenth of November last, with a temporary increase of fifty per cent. from the said fifteenth day of November; such compensation hereby allowed to be in lieu of all other allowances; it being understood, however, that this action is not to be considered as enacting any rule for the compensation of the successors of such officers.

1873, Nov. 3.
$200 to Mr. Weeks.
Resolved, That the sum of two hundred dollars be allowed to the Janitor of the College, Mr. Weeks, in addition to his regular salary for the present financial year, the same to be paid at such times and in such instalments as provided for the payment of similar allowances heretofore.

1873, Nov. 3.
Temporary augmentation of salaries.

Resolved, That the provisions of the resolutions of January 6th, 1868, granting a temporary increase of salary and compensation of fifty per cent. upon the salaries of the President, Professors, and other officers and persons therein named, to be computed upon the salaries as now established, be continued in force from the fifteenth of November, 1873, until the further order of this Board; and that the benefits of this resolution be made applicable to Professor Short and the Librarian.

1873, Dec. 1.
Treasurer to have a Clerk.

Resolved, That the Treasurer be authorized to employ a competent clerk, at a salary of not more than fifteen hundred dollars, the salary paid to be accounted for in the usual course of such disbursements.

SCHOLARSHIPS, FREE.

1870, Feb 7
Free Scholarships

Resolved, That the President be requested, in all advertisements of the College and of the School of Mines, and in every annual Catalogue, to state the liberal terms upon which this institution admits students in either of such departments free of charge.

SEAL.

1870, Nov. 7.
To be signed and sealed.

Resolved, That the Clerk be authorized to sign, and affix the corporate seal to all instruments necessary to carry into effect the last preceding resolution.

1870, Dec. 5.
To be sealed.

Resolved, That the Clerk be authorized to furnish to the Treasurer, a certified copy of the last preceding resolution attested by the corporate seal.

1871, Nov. 6. Seal.	Also *Resolved*, That the Clerk be authorized to sign and affix the corporate seal to any instrument proper to release, discharged from such rent, the lots of land now charged with it.
1871, Nov. 6. Seal.	Also, *Resolved*, That the Clerk be authorized to sign and affix the corporate seal to all leases granted by the Standing Committee under the last preceding resolution.
1872, Oct. 22.	*Resolved*, That the Clerk be authorized to sign and affix the corporate seal to any instruments in writing necessary or expedient to carry into effect the preceding resolutions.
1873, June 2. Clerk to sign and seal.	*Resolved*, That the Clerk be authorized to sign and affix the corporate seal to any proper and usual instruments in writing on behalf of this Corporation, acknowledging the receipt of either or both such awards, and releasing to the Corporation of the city of New York the lands taken for either or both the said improvements; also,
To furnish copies.	*Resolved*, That the Clerk be authorized to furnish to the Treasurer a copy or copies of the last two preceding resolutions, attested under the corporate seal.

SITE, COMMITTEE ON THE.

1869, March 1. Committee on location of College.	The committee to whom was referred that part of the last Annual Report of the president of the college relating to a new location and permanent site of the college, beg leave to report—
	That, having considered the subject, they are of the opinion that it is not expedient for the board of trustees to take any action thereon at the present time.
Action of Board as to locating College.	*Resolved*, That it is not expedient that the board of trustees take any action at the present time on the subject of a new location and permanent site of the college.

SITE, COMMITTEE ON THE.

1869, May 3.
Committee on site of College.

Resolved, That the committee on a new location and permanent site of the college be requested to make a further report in June; and that such report be made the special order.

1871, Nov. 6.
Committee on Site to report

Resolved, That the Committee on the Site of the College be requested to report at the next meeting.

1871, Dec. 4.

The Committee on the Site recommended to the Board of Trustees the following resolutions for their adoption:

Resolved, That in the opinion of this Board it is expedient to take immediate steps to secure a site of at least twice the dimensions of the one now occupied by the College, with a view to the ultimate removal thither of the institution.

Resolved, That it is deemed inexpedient to lay out any considerable sums of money in erecting additional buildings on the present site.

1872, April 1.

Proposed resolutions appended to the report.

" *Resolved*, That the Committe on a New Site be authorized to make a purchase on behalf of this Corporation of any lands in the City of New York, of an area not less than 800 feet by 200 feet, at a cost not exceeding five hundred thousand dollars; and to direct the execution under the corporate seal of a contract for such purpose; or for the assumption of such a contract if made by any other party.

1872, Oct. 22.
Resolutions.

Resolved, That the property thirdly described in the report of the Committee on a New Site now under consideration, be provisionally secured for the future site of the college, subject to the ultimate decision of this Board whether it shall be finally adopted as such site.

Resolved, That the Committee on a New Site, if they

shall deem such a measure expedient for the purpose of carrying out the last preceding resolution, shall have power, should such property be purchased by and be conveyed in fee simple to three persons, approved by the Committee as joint tenants, and not as tenants in common, to direct the Treasurer to loan to such persons the whole purchase money, receiving from them a mortgage to this corporation of the said property, without covenants and without bond, to secure said purchase money with interest at seven per cent. per annum, together with all amounts which shall be paid by the college for taxes, assessments, and insurances, and for examining title and conveyancing, and that the Committee shall also have power to make such other stipulations and agreements as shall more effectually secure the interests of the college.

Also *Resolved*, That all the powers heretofore granted for raising funds to be applied to the purchase of a site shall be applicable to, and be exercised for, the purpose of raising funds for such loan should the same be made.

1872, Nov. 4.
Title to the Wheelock property.

Resolved, That the Committee on the Site have discretion to authorize the acceptance of the title to the Wheelock property, notwithstanding the existence of a question as to the title to a small piece of land on the northerly side of said property, which question is in course of settlement by suit.

1873, Nov. 3.
Enlarged accommodations referred to Committee on Site.

Resolved, That it be referred to the Committee on the Site of the College to inquire and report what measures ought to be taken to enlarge the accommodations for instruction in the School of Mines and in the college, and that said Committee report to this Board at the stated meeting in December next.

1873, Dec. 22.
$150,000 appropriated to improve the College buildings.

Resolved, That the subject be referred back to the Committee, and that they be authorized to make alterations and additions to the present buildings on the present site of the College, at a cost not to exceed one hundred and fifty thousand dollars.

STATUTES, COMMITTEE ON.

<small>1869, Feb. 1.
Special Committee on Statutes.</small>

Resolved, That it be referred to a special committee of five to inquire and report whether any modification of the statutes of the college is advisable in regard, first, to the mode of enforcing regularity of attendance in the scholastic and religious exercises of the college; and, secondly, to the mode of determining the standing, relative and absolute, of the students of the several classes in general scholarship and in the merit rolls of the different departments; thirdly, to the general system of discipline in the college, embracing the entire subject of offences and their penalties. President Barnard, Dr. Haight, Mr. Strong, Judge Blatchford, and Mr. Jones were appointed the committee.

<small>1869, Feb. 1.
Communication from Seniors.</small>

A communication from the senior class, asking that the system of marks be abolished, was referred to the same committee, with power to grant the request should they deem it advisable.

<small>1869, March 1.
Report of Committee on the Statutes.</small>

The committee of the trustees of Columbia College, appointed to inquire into the expediency of modifying the statutes of the college, in relation to the subjects of attendance, discipline, and the determination of standing in scholarship, and also to consider whether it is advisable in the meantime temporarily to suspend the operation of any portion of the said statutes, with power to act in their discretion on the matter last named, believing that a simplification of the code would be attended with good results, have resolved, and in the exercise of the power conferred upon them, do resolve as follows:

I. As to Discipline.

<small>1869, March 1.
Discipline.</small>

From and after the 18th day of February instant, and until the further order of this committee, or of the board of trustees, all those portions of the college statutes and

STATUTES, COMMITTEE ON. 63

by-laws which relate to discipline, viz.: the final clause of Section 2, Chapter IV., the whole of Chapter V., the whole of Chapter VI., and the whole of Chapter VII. of the statutes, and Chapters I. and III. of the by-laws, shall be suspended in their operation, and in lieu thereof the following provisions shall be in force as the rule of government of the college :

1. Any case of misconduct in a student shall be referred in the first instance to the president, who shall hear the student's own statement in private, and shall admonish him, if necessary, in like manner.

2. In case any member of a class under instruction disturb the class exercises, the professor presiding may require such student to leave the room, and the student thereupon shall report himself to the president.

3. Such rules of order as may be required to secure regularity, and to prevent confusion in the operations of the college, shall be announced by the faculty. These, it is presumed, will be complied with from their obvious necessity and fitness; but should they be persistently disregarded by any student, the board of the college may require such student to cease from attendance at the college. This provision shall apply also to persistency in the cases provided for in Regulations 1 and 2.

II. AS TO SCHOLARSHIP.

1869, March 1.
Scholarship.

From and after the 18th day of February instant, aforesaid, and until further order, as aforesaid, Chapter X. of the statutes relating to the proficiency of the students and to the mode of estimating standing in scholarship, and Chapter II. of the by-laws, shall be suspended in their operations; and hereafter standing in scholarship, whether absolute or relative, shall be determined only by the results of the examinations provided for in Chapter IX. of the statutes; which examinations shall be conducted in accordance with the following principles :

(I.) The examinations shall be, so far as possible, in writing.

(II.) The examination papers previously prepared by the professors shall not exact more than a good scholar may reasonably be expected to perform within the time allotted.

(III.) Each question, topic, passage for translation or analysis, problem or proposition in mathematics, or other separate head of exaction, shall have a valuation put upon it in advance, which shall be the value awarded for a perfect performance; inferior performances, shall receive lower valuations, according to the estimate of their merit by the examining officer.

(IV.) The exactions made in the examination papers shall be the same for every student of the class under examination.

(V.) If there are any exercises, as of pronunciation, declamation, etc., which from their nature cannot be performed in writing, the exactions from each student shall be as nearly identical as possible.

(VI.) The sum total of all the valuations assigned to the performances of each student in any department shall be taken to express the value of the student's scholarship in said department, and an order of merit shall be prepared accordingly. An order of merit in general scholarship shall be prepared by combining the values expressive of scholarship in the several departments.

Should the Board of Trustees see fit to make permanent the system here established provisionally, an order of merit shall be formed after each successive examination by adding the results of the same to the sum of the results of preceding examinations.

Immediately after the preparation of the orders of merit above provided, the numerical values expressive of the merit of each student in scholarship in each department, shall be posted in the college, and such values as to each student shall be communicated to his parents.

Classes of honor shall continue to be distinguished as heretofore. The Faculty are required to prepare and submit to the Board of Trustees a plan for making such distinctions which shall be in harmony with these provisions.

Students found deficient either at the intermediate or at the final examination, may, in the discretion of the Faculty, be dropped from the roll; but in no event shall they be eligible to graduation at the end of the course unless their deficiency shall have been satisfactorily made good.

The professors in the several departments shall make monthly returns to the president of the standing of the students in their departments, according to their best judgment, arranging *them* as at present in classes numbering from 1 to 5; of which numbers No. 1 shall mean the highest in the order of merit, and No. 5 the lowest. Nos. 1, 2, and 3 being classes of honor.

1869, April 5. Modification of programme of instruction. *Resolved*, That the Committee on the Statutes be instructed to inquire whether it is advisable to make any modification in the arrangement of the programme of instruction in the college; and whether it would affect advantageously or otherwise the interests of the college, or the School of Mines, to confine Professor Peck's instructions entirely to the college.

1869, June 7. Order of studies. Optional studies. *Resolved*, That the Committee on the Statutes be instructed to inquire and report whether any change is advisable in the order in which the different studies are now taught in the undergraduate course, in the distribution of time among the several departments, and in the extent to which studies may be made optional, and that to this end they confer with the president and the Board of the College and make report at the next meeting of this Board.

1870, Feb. 7.
Examinations.

Resolved, That it be referred to the Committee on the Statutes to consider and report upon the expediency of adopting such amendments to the statute regulations concerning examinations as may tend to guard against an undue valuation of the performances of students who resort to prohibited means of assistance.

1870, April 4.
Statutes.

Resolved, That it be referred to the Committee on the Statutes to prepare and submit to this Board permanent statutes in respect to discipline, scholarship, and attendance, to go into effect on the first day of October next.

Resolved, That the same committee consider and report upon the expediency of inserting in the statutes a provision that no student shall be allowed to continue in the College if he shall commence any professional study during his academical course.

III. As to Attendance.

1869, March 1.
Attendance.

Record shall be kept, as at present, of the attendance of students upon the religious and scholastic exercises of the college. A student who shall have been absent for more than one quarter of the total number of exercises in any department shall not be admitted to examination in that department, unless in case of a continuous absence owing to serious illness or other cause beyond the student's control.

Tardiness of attendance shall be estimated as equivalent to one half an absence. When a student leaves a class-room during an exercise, and fails to return before the close of the exercise in time to perform his part, his egression shall be counted as an absence, unless he shall have performed before going out.

Every parent or guardian of a student shall be furnished monthly with a statement of the attendance of such student, unless a wish to the contrary shall be communicated to the president.

STATUTES, COMMITTEE ON THE. 67

Printed copies of resolutions.   The president shall immediatly send printed copies of these resolutions to the parents and guardians of all the students.

1870, May 2. Voluntary studies.   *Resolved*, That it be referred to the Committee on Statutes to inquire whether it may not be expedient and practicable so to modify the system of instruction in the College as to allow to the students of the Junior and Senior Classes some larger latitude of choice in regard to the studies pursued by them during the last two years of the course; and in case of an affirmative decision, to report to the Trustees a scheme of instruction by which that object may be accomplished.

1872, March 2.   *Resolved*, That it be referred to the Committee on the Statutes to consider and report whether it is not expedient to change the day for holding the annual Commencement.

1872, April 1. Chapter 3 of the Statutes amended.   *Resolved*, That Chapter III. of the Statutes be amended by striking out the words "Analytical Geometry" where they occur in § 3, and inserting the same after the word "History" in § 4.

1872, April 1. Report of Committee on Statutes.   The Committee on the Statutes, to whom was referred the resolution offered by the President proposing that the words "Analytical Geometry" be stricken out, § 3, Chapter III., and inserted after the word "History" in § 4 of the same chapter, have considered the subject referred to them, and concur in recommending the adoption of the resolution.

1872, June 3. Statute about examinations referred to Committee on Statutes.   *Resolved*, That the resolution of the Board of the College, recorded in the minutes of the proceedings of the Board of Friday, May 31st, proposing that honor examinations be held in the Freshman, Sophomore, and Junior Classes, as well as in the Senior, together with the amendment to the Statutes proposed at the last meeting of the Trustees, relating to the intermediate examination, be referred to the Committee on the Statutes, with instructions to inquire and report on the whole subject of examinations at the stated meeting of the Trustees to be held in November next.

STANDING COMMITTEE.

<small>1868, Feb. 6.
Lot 111, 48th street.</small>   *Resolved*, That Mr. John C. Calhoun, the lessee of Lot 111, 48th street, have leave to surrender his lease, the rents, taxes, charges and assessments being previously paid; and that a new lease be given to him for the same lot, at the same rent as the present lease, the term and rent to commence on the first day of February instant.

<small>Authority to Clerk.</small>   *Resolved*, That the clerk have authority to affix the corporate seal to the necessary papers.

<small>1868. May 4.
Rents unpaid for over 6 months.</small>   *Resolved*, That in all cases in which rents for more than six months, payable by leases granted by the college, are now unpaid, the standing committee shall have power to direct the prosecution of such suits or proceedings to enforce the rights of the college, grounded upon any of the provisions of the leases as shall appear to them to be expedient.

<small>1868, Oct. 5.
Resolution on judgment in case of lot 135, 49th street.</small>   *Resolved*, That the judgment recovered to put the college in possession of the lot number 135, in Forty-ninth street, be vacated, and the consent of the college given under its seal to the assignment of the lease of such lot to John L. Smith, or other party approved by the standing committee; provided, however, that on or before the 15th October, 1868, payment shall be made to the treasurer, of the rent up to the first day of November next, with interest on the arrears of all taxes and assessments then due, and of the expenses of the suit in which such judgment was recovered.

<small>1868, Oct. 5.
New lease of lot 300, Murray str't.</small>   *Resolved*, That the standing committee have power to grant a new lease of lot known as number 300 in Murray street, upon such terms as regards the ownership of the building upon the lot, and otherwise, as the committee may deem expedient, to which lease the seal of the college shall be affixed, and the same shall be signed by the clerk.

1868, Nov. 2. Rents unpaid.	*Resolved,* That in all cases in which rents for more than six months are now unpaid, the standing committee shall have power to direct the prosecution of such suits or proceedings as they may deem expedient to enforce the rights of the college, grounded upon any of the provisions of the leases by which such rents are reserved.
1868, Nov. 2. U. S. Stocks.	*Resolved,* That the standing committee have power to invest in any of the stocks of the United States such part of the funds of the college as may be at any time within the present financial year in the treasurer's hands, and as will probably not be required to meet the expenses of the year, with power to direct the sale of such stock if it shall appear to be expedient.
1868, Nov. 2. Application of S. R. Van Duzer.	*Resolved,* That the application of Selah R. Van Duzer, proposing to surrender the pending leases of lots 207 in Barclay street, and 207 A in Park place, and to take a new renewable lease of the same, be referred to the standing committee with power, should they deem it expedient to accept such surrender and grant such new lease upon such terms as they shall judge to be proper; and that the clerk be authorized to sign and affix the corporate seal to any lease that may be authorized by the committee under this resolution.
1868, Dec. 7. Application of S. A. Buckley and E. C. Crocker.	*Resolved,* That the application of Sarah A. Buckley and Eliza C. Crocker, for an extension of the time to build under the lease of lot 217–218 A, in Greenwich street, be referred to the standing committee, with power to extend such time for such period as they shall think expedient, and to authorize the execution under the corporate seal of such instruments as may be proper in the premises.
1869, Feb. 1. Leases of lots.	*Resolved,* That the standing committee have power to direct the acceptance of the surrender of any or all of the leases of lots numbers 202 and 203 in Barclay street, 202 A and 203 A in Park Place, and 295 and 296 in College Place, and the granting of new leases of the same lots to the holders of the existing leases, upon such terms as the

committee may deem expedient; to which new leases, if sanctioned by such committee, the corporal seal shall be affixed.

1869, Feb. 1.
Application Presbyterian Church.

The standing committee, to whom had been referred an application in relation to building a Presbyterian church upon the college ground, reported the following resolution, which was adopted:

1869, Feb. 1.
Leases.

Resolved, That, inasmuch as all the leases of the college contemplate the erection of dwelling-houses, and have been taken by the tenants with that understanding, it would be inconsiderate with that *understanding* to comply with the request of the church.

1869, Feb. 1.
Alterations President's house.

Resolved, That the bill of charges for alterations in the president's house, and in the manner of warming the same, and for the renewal of the kitchen range, be referred to the standing committee with power.

1869, Mar. 1.
Lease to J. & T. Stevenson.

Resolved, That the clerk be authorized to re-execute, under the corporate seal, a lease heretofore executed to John Stevenson and Thomas Stevenson, of the lot in Fiftieth street, designated on the college map by the number two hundred and thirty-three, the original lease having been lost and not having been recorded.

1869, Apr. 5.
Lease of 37 Lafayette Place.

Resolved, That the clerk be authorized to execute and affix the corporate seal to a lease of the premises No. 37 Lafayette place, which have been hired for the Law School, under the direction of the law committee, for one year from the first day of May next, at the same rent now paid.

1869, June 7.
Party wall, lots 110 and 109.

Resolved, That the Standing Committee be authorized to make an agreement under seal with the holders of leases of lots 109 and 110 Forty-eighth street, that a 16-inch wall erected wholly on lot No. 110, shall be a party wall between such lots during the continuance of the existing terms and of any future term granted under either lease.

1869, Nov. 1. Dr. Trenor's lease	*Resolved*, That the standing committee be authorized to accept from Dr. John Trenor the surrender of his lease of the lot 291 in College Place, and to grant to him a new original lease, in the usual form, of the same property, the rent for the first term of twenty-one years, from the 1st of May, 1869, to be $750 per annum, until May 1st, 1872, when the present term will expire, and thereafter $1,550 per annum; and that the clerk sign the new lease and seal it with the seal of the college.
1869, Nov. 1. Leases of lots. Power to Committee.	*Resolved*, That in relation to leases of lots numbers 40, 42, 44 and 46 in Murray street, which will expire on the first day of May next, and in relation to lease of lot 38, in Murray street, which will expire on the first day of November next, the standing committee have power to agree, on the part of the college, for a renewal of the lease, respectively, and thereupon to grant renewal leases; and that in case of disagreement as to the terms of renewal, the committee have power to nominate appraisers to value the buildings, and to determine what would be reasonable yearly rent on renewal; that the committee also have power, upon any report of appraisers, to elect, on the part of the college, to grant a new lease or to pay for the value of the buildings on the lot leased. Also,
	Resolved, That, in the event of the committee electing to pay for buildings under the last preceding resolution, they have authority to raise the sum necessary to make such payment, upon bond or notes of this corporation, to be issued under the direction of the committee. Also,
	Resolved, That the corporate seal be affixed to any leases and other papers necessary or proper to carry out the last two preceding resolutions.
1869, Nov. 1. Application of Mercer street Church.	*Resolved*, That the application of the Mercer street church be granted, subject to such special provisions and restrictions in the new leases, as the standing committee may deem it necessary to require for the protection of the interests of this corporation.

A Memorial from the Trustees of the Mercer street Church, asking a modification of the conditions of a lease proposed to be given to said church, being under consideration,

1869, Dec. 6.
Mercer street Church.

Resolved, That the application of the Mercer street church be declined; and that the consent to grant a lease to them be rescinded.

On motion of the treasurer:

1869, Dec. 6.
Leases of lots in upper estate.

Resolved, That the standing committee have power to make, from time to time, with lessees of lots in the upper estate, such modifications of their leases, in respect to their time for building, as shall appear to the committee to be expedient, and that the clerk affix the seal of the corporation to all instruments, in writing, which may be authorized by the committee under this resolution.

1870, Jan. 3.
Widening of Robinson street.

Resolved, That it be referred to the Standing Committee to consider the expediency of objecting at the hearing of the application to confirm the report of the Commissioners of Estimate and Assessment in the matter of the widening of Robinson street, to further proceedings upon the said report; also,

Resolved, That if the Committee deem such course expedient the Treasurer be authorized to make such objection in the name of, and on behalf of this corporation.

1870, March 7.
Application of Mr. A. Higgins.

On motion of the Treasurer, after considering an application of Mr. Alvin Higgins for a renewal of the lease of the lot known on the College map as the north half of lot No. 180 in Church street:

Declined.

Resolved, That it is inexpedient at this time to treat for such a renewal, or to determine what disposition should be made of the lot in question on the termination of the existing lease thereof.

STANDING COMMITTEE. 73

1870, March. 7.
Lease of No. 37 Lafayette Place to be sealed.

Resolved, That the Clerk be authorized to sign and affix the Corporate Seal to a lease to the College for one year from the 1st May next, of premises No. 37 Lafayette Place, for the use of the Law School, such lease having been concluded under the direction of the Law Committee.

1870, October.
S. Mason, application for license to make soap, referred.

Resolved, That it be referred to the Standing Committee to consider the expediency of granting a license to the lessee of lots 214, 215, and 217, 218 B, in College Place and Robinson street, to use such premises or part of the same for the manufacture of toilet soaps; and if deemed by them to be expedient, with power to grant such license and to authorize the affixing thereto of the corporate seal.

1870, Nov. 7.
Renewal of down town leases referred to Standing Committee.

Resolved, That the Standing Committee have authority to agree for, and authorize the execution of renewal leases of the lots known by the college map numbers 36 in Murray street, IV. in Murray street, and VII. in Greenwich street; also to agree for, and authorize the execution of original renewable leases in the usual form, of lots known by the college map numbers V., VI., 1, 2, 3, 4, 5, 6, 308, 309, 310, and 311 in Greenwich street, and 312 in Robinson street, also to extend the occupancy of the lessees, and under-lessees, to the thirteen lots last above mentioned, from the first day of September, 1871, when the existing leases thereof will expire, until the first day of May next succeeding, upon such terms as the committee shall deem proper.

1870, Dec. 5.

Resolved, That the action of the Standing Committee declining the application of Mr. C. H. Day, the Librarian and Register of the School of Mines, for an increase of salary, be approved.

Authorized to commence suits.

The action of the same committee, authorizing the Treasurer to commence suits to annul the leases of certain lots, for an alleged violation of the covenants therein contained, in constructing improper roofs on the buildings, was approved.

<small>1870, Dec. 5. Mr. Hagadorn and others, application declined.</small>
The action of the same committee declining the application of Mr. Hagadorn and others for a modification of the leases of certain lots on Fifth avenue, between 50th and 51st streets, to enable them to erect houses of a high character, for themselves and others as apartment houses, was approved.

<small>1870, Dec. 19.</small>

<small>Leases, Greenwich street lots.</small>
Resolved, That the Standing Committee have authority to grant original renewable leases upon such terms as they shall deem desirable for the interest of the college, of the lots in Greenwich street, known on the College Map by the numbers 219 and 220, the existing lease of which will expire on the eleventh day of January, 1872; and also to grant a lease, or leases, upon such terms as they shall consider expedient, of the same property from the said eleventh day of January to the next succeeding first day of May.

<small>1871, Feb. 6. Lease, lots IV. and VII.</small>
Resolved, That the Standing Committee have power to accept the surrender of the existing leases of the two lots known on the College Map by the numbers IV. and VII., and to lease the same, with or without other adjoining lots, upon such terms as the Committee shall deem to be for the interest of the college, and that the seal of the college be affixed to all instruments proper in the premises.

<small>1871, May 1,</small>
The recommendation of the Standing Committee on paving Madison avenue and Fiftieth street was approved, with an addition as follows:

<small>Paving Madison avenue and 50th street.</small>
That the Trustees authorize the Treasurer, under the direction of the Standing Committee, to procure the sidewalk on Madison avenue, opposite the college grounds, and likewise the sidewalk in 50th street, opposite the college grounds, to be paved the requisite width; and to make such application as may be necessary for permis-

sion for the college to do the work at its own expense; also, that the Standing Committee have power to remove the face of the rock on 50th street, under the college building, as far as may seem to them to be requisite; or to adopt such other measures for the better appearance and repair of the front of the college building on that street as they shall judge expedient.

1871, May 1.
Mrs Vanderpoel and Mrs.McLanahan, leases, &c.

Resolved, That the application of Mrs. Vanderpoel and Mrs. McLanahan, in relation to the rebuilding the front of a store on lot 312, in Robinson street, which is to be taken for the widening of that street, be referred to the Standing Committee, with power to make such agreement as to the ownership of said building, and the terms of a new lease or leases of the said lot, as to the Committee shall seem expedient.

1871, June 5.
Lots 308 and 309 Greenwich street.

It appearing that owing to the non-residence and want of responsibility of the holder of the lease of the lots 30 and 309 in Greenwich street (which will expire on the first day of November next), the college will be obliged to pay the assessments imposed upon such lots for the extension of Park Place: *Resolved*, That the Standing Committee be authorized to make any agreement they shall deem proper with the under-lessee of such lots, for the payment to the college of the rent reserved by the underlease to him and for his indemnity; and to that end, if thought expedient, to assign to him the claim of the college against the holder of the original lease, growing out of the payment of the said assessment; also, that the Clerk be authorized to execute and affix the corporate seal to any instrument proper in the premises.

1871, June 5.
Overflow in wing of College.

Resolved, That it be referred to the Standing Committee to inquire into the nature and causes of the damage occasioned by an overflow of water in the northwest wing of the college building during the winter; and to consider where the responsibility for the injury should rest: with power to defray the expense of the same out of the treasury of the college, if it should appear that the college ought to be charged with it.

<small>1871, Oct. 2.
Reduction of fees referred to Standing Committee.</small>
Resolved, That it be referred to the Standing Committee to ascertain and report what, if any, reduction of the tuition fees of the College and School of Mines is expedient, and when such reduction (if any such be recommended) should go into effect.

<small>1871, Nov. 6.
Renewal of leases.</small>
Resolved, That the Standing Committee have power to grant renewal leases, or original renewable leases, in the usual form, of the lots specified in the following list, the leases of which will expire on the first day of May, 1872, that is to say:

Lot 180 in Barclay street.
" 198 and 198 A, in Park place and Barclay street.
" 199 and 199 A,   "   "   "
" 200 in Barclay street.
" 200 A and 201 A, in Park place.
" 212 in Barclay street.
" 213 in College place.
" 214 ⎫
" 215 ⎬ in College place.
" 217 ⎪
" 218 B ⎭
" 292 in College place.
" 293, 294 "   "
" 295, 296 "   "
" 297   "   "

<small>1871, Dec. 4.</small>
Resolved, That it be referred to the Standing Committee, with power to take the necessary measures to obtain the requisite authority to acquire and hold such land as may be necessary for buildings for the site of this college.

<small>1871, Dec. 4.</small>
Resolved, That the existing Committee on the Site be continued, and that they be directed to take measures, with all convenient dispatch, to find a suitable location

STANDING COMMITTEE. 77

for the college as contemplated by the first of the foregoing resolutions.

1872, Jan. 2.
Standing Committee to inquire about making contributions to Sewanee University.

Resolved, That it be referred to the Standing Committee to inquire whether it is possible, consistently with the interests of this college, to make any contribution to the scientific apparatus or collections in mineralogy or geology of Sewanee University, with power to authorize any such contributions as in their judgment may with propriety be made.

1872, Mar. 2.
Standing Committee to appoint appraisers.

Resolved, That in every case of a lease expiring on the first day of May, 1872, containing covenants of renewal, the Standing Committee have authority to direct the nomination and appointment on the part of this Corporation, by an instrument to be executed under the corporate seal, of a fit and impartial person to value the building standing upon the lot demised by such lease, and also to determine what would be a reasonable yearly rent for the said lot, or in case part thereof shall have been taken for the widening of a street, then for the residue of such lot, during a further term of twenty-one years from the said first day of May.

1872, May 6.
Lease of lot 179 Barclay street.

Seal.

Resolved, That the Standing Committee have power to accept a surrender of the existing lease of lot known by the map number 179 in Barclay street, and to grant a new lease of the same, in the usual form of original renewable leases of lots in the lower estate, upon such rent as shall be agreed upon ; and the Clerk is authorized to sign and affix the corporate seal to such lease as may be granted under this resolution.

1872, June, 3.
Painting the College Buildings.

Resolved, That the Standing Committee, after conferring with the President, be authorized to contract for the painting of the exterior of the college buildings, including the School of Mines (walls and woodwork being included), on all sides of the same, and of the house occupied by the Janitor, with two good coats of paint, of such color as may be adjudged best by the Committee, at an expense not to exceed three thousand dollars; or in case they shall deem it advisable to paint only the woodwork, and to apply to the walls the patent wash proposed by Mr. Livingston, that they be authorized to cause the work to be done at an expense not exceeding fifteen hundred dollars.

1873, Jan. 6.
Representation at Vienna Exposition, referred to Standing Committee.

Resolved, That it be referred to the Standing Committee to inquire and report as to the expediency of taking measures to secure a representation of Columbia College at the Vienna Exposition, on the plan presented in the letter of the Commissioners of Education, and recommended by the Board of the College.

1873, Feb. 3.
Leases in Barclay street.

Resolved, That the Standing Committee have power to negotiate for, and conclude agreements, for leases of the lots known on the college map by the numbers 210 in Barclay street; and 208, 208A in Barclay street, for terms commencing with the expirations of the terms of the existing leases, at such rents and under such covenants and conditions as shall appear to the committee to be expedient; to which new leases, when authorized by the committee, the seal of the college shall be affixed.

1873, May 5.
Painting and repairing the College.

Resolved, That the Standing Committee be instructed to inquire and report whether it is advisable to improve the exterior of the college building by paint or color-washing; and also, what other improvements may be necessary about the buildings of the college and School of Mines before the commencement of another academic year.

1873, June 2.
Standing Committee to direct repairs in the College.

Resolved, That the Standing Committee have power to direct such improvements and repairs in the college buildings and the School of Mines as they shall deem necessary.

Not to paint.

Resolved, That it is not expedient to improve the exterior of the college buildings by paint or color-washing.

STANDING COMMITTEE.   79

1873, Oct. 6.
Contract with
Joseph D. Beers.

Resolved, That it be referred to the Standing Committee to inquire whether, in respect to the lot of land on the north-east corner of 50th street and the Sixth avenue, any breach has been committed in any of the covenants contained in a certain agreement made the 25th day of July, 1859, between this corporation and Joseph D. Beers; with power to take such measures in the name of this corporation, by suit or otherwise, as the Committee shall deem expedient in consequence of such breach, if any have been made.

1873, Nov 3.
New leases in
Barclay street.

Resolved, That the Standing Committee have power to grant original renewable leases, upon such terms as it shall deem expedient, of lots the leases of which will expire on the first day of May, 1874, that is to say, of the lots known by the map numbers 177, 178, and 179 in Barclay street, and 1 in Park Place, and to authorize the execution, under the corporate seal, of such leases; also,

Resolved, That the same Committee shall be authorized, if it shall deem it expedient, to direct the appointment, under the corporate seal, under the provisions of the lease of the said lot 1 in Park Place, of a person to value the store upon such lot, and to determine what would be a reasonable rent for a new term of twenty-one years.

Advances to the
Dean of the
School of Mines.

Resolved, That the Standing Committee have power to authorize the increase of the amount which may be advanced by the Treasurer to the Dean of the School of Mines, under resolutions of this Board passed on the eighteenth day of December, 1865.

1873, Nov. 3.
Mr. Waldo's Salary.

Resolved, That it be referred to the Standing Committee to inquire and report as to the expediency of increasing the salary of Mr. Waldo, or otherwise providing, so as to enable him to accept the invitation of Admiral Sands to accompany one of the expeditions sent out by the United States to observe the Transit of Venus in 1874.

STUDENTS.

1868, Oct. 5.
Dr. C. A. Bacon's case.
Resolved, That Dr. Charles A. Bacon, an alumnus of the college of the year 1855, be permitted to attend the lectures given to the senior class on optics, provided the consent of the professor in that department be first obtained, and during the pleasure of this board.

1870, May 2.
W. L. Murphy.
Resolved, That William L. Murphy, a member of the Sophomore Class now in College, be permitted to discontinue attendance in the department of Mathematics, and that he cease at the same time to be regarded as a candidate for a degree in Arts.

1870, Nov. 7.
C C. Merriam to attend Prof. Rood in College.
Resolved, That Charles Collins Merriam, a member of the School of Mines, pursuing a partial course of instruction, be permitted, in consequence of the peculiar circumstances of his case, to attend the lectures and other exercises given by Prof. Rood, to the Senior Class in College, in addition to those which he now attends with the same officer, along with the preparatory class in the School of Mines.

1873, Jan. 6.
Mr. A. F. Smith's application granted.
Resolved, That the request of A. Foster Smith, for leave to discontinue for the present the study of mathematics and of Greek, be granted.

TREASURER.

1868, Feb. 6.
U. S. Certificates.
Resolved, That Gouverneur M. Ogden, the treasurer of the trustees of Columbia College, in the city of New York, have authority to sell and assign from time to time, as occasion may require, the certificate or certificates of any United States stock standing in the name of this corporation.

TREASURER.   81

Certified copy of preceding resolution. *Resolved*, That the clerk be authorized to furnish to the treasurer a certified copy of the last preceding resolution, from time to time, when authorized to do so by the standing committee, to which the seal of this corporation shall be affixed.

1868, Oct. 5. Authorization of Treasurer to employ Attorney. *Resolved*, That the treasurer be authorized to employ an attorney to appear for the college in the action of John M. Knox, executor of Alfred G. Jones *vs.* William B. Jones, and others, for the construction of a will.

1868, Dec. 7. Profs. Chandler and Newberry. Ives's case. *Resolved*, That the treasurer be authorized to pay to Professors Chandler and Newberry $166.66 for the salary to the 15th November last, of J. C. Ives, now deceased, lately an assistant in the School of Mines, such professors having advanced to him that amount upon an agreement that they were to retain such advance out of his salary, upon their executing an agreement to hold the college harmless.

1869, April 5. Appropriation advanced to Prof. Egleston. *Resolved*, That the treasurer be authorized to advance to Prof. Egleston such proportions of the sums which may be appropriated for the uses of the departments of instruction under his care, for the financial year 1869–70 as he may desire, not exceeding four-fifths of the same, to be expended by him for the benefit of said departments during the summer of 1869; and also that he be authorized to advance to the same professor a sum not exceeding one-third of the amount which may be appropriated for the uses of the library of the School of Mines for the same financial year, to be in like manner expended by him for the benefit of said library.

1869, May 3. Payment of College bonds. *Resolved*, That in order to provide for the payment of the bonds of the college to the New York Life Insurance and Trust Company, in all for $3,500, falling due in July, August, and September next, the treasurer be authorized to apply to such purpose, under the direction of the standing committee, so much of the accumulating fund as will suffice to make such payment after the application to the same purpose of such part of the general income as may not be required for current expenses; and that to that end the treasurer be authorized to sell and assign, under the like direction, so much of the United States stocks belonging to such fund as it may be necessary to sell to make such payment.

<small>1869, Dec. 6.
Investments by Treasurer.</small>
Resolved, That the treasurer be authorized to invest, from time to time, under the direction of the standing committee, in Stocks of the United States, or of the State of New York, or of the City of New York, any moneys that, in the judgment of the committee, will probably not be required for the expenditures of the year in which such investment shall be made; and also, if it seem to the standing committee to be necessary to convert into money the investments made under this resolution, or any part of them, and to assign any securities held for the same; and that the clerk affix the corporate seal to any papers necessary in the premises.

<small>1870, Jan. 3.
Mr. Kemble's portrait.</small>
Resolved, That the Treasurer be authorized to pay the sum of fifty dollars, or so much thereof as may be necessary, to be charged to the contingency fund of the School of Mines, to reimburse Dr. Torrey for money advanced by him in payment for a photograph portrait of the Hon. Gouverneur Kemble, now in the mineralogical cabinet of the School of Mines, and that the said portrait be hereafter permanently preserved in said cabinet.

<small>1870, May 2
Leave of absence to the Treasurer.</small>
Leave of absence was granted to the Treasurer from the twenty-second of June to the first day of October, 1870.

<small>Acting Treasurer.</small>
Resolved, That George D. L. Harison is hereby appointed acting Treasurer of this Corporation to perform the duties of that office during the leave of absence of the Treasurer, that is to say, from the twenty-second day of June, 1870, to the first day of October, 1870.

TREASURER. 83

Resolved, That George D. L. Harison, as acting Treasurer, be authorized to receive, from time to time, as it shall accrue, the interest on any stock, bonds, or evidences of indebtedness of the United States, or of the State of New York, standing in the name of this Corporation, such interest falling due between the twenty-second day of June, 1870, and the first day of October, 1870.

Resolved, That the Clerk be authorized to furnish to Mr. George D. L. Harison copies of the foregoing resolutions from time to time as may be expedient, and to affix thereto the corporate seal.

1870, May 2.
$400 to Prof. Egleston for School of Mines Library.

Resolved, That the Treasurer be authorized to advance to Prof. Egleston the sum of four hundred dollars out of the appropriation made for the library of the School of Mines for the financial year commencing October 1, 1870, to be expended by him in Europe for the increase of the library of the School during the ensuing summer.

1870, Nov. 7.
Power of Attorney to collect interest on U. S. stock.

Resolved, That the Clerk be authorized to execute under the corporate seal, a proper instrument to appoint some person or persons, the attorney or attorneys of this corporation, to receive from the proper officer, all interest due on the first day of September, one thousand eight hundred and seventy, on all stock standing in the name of this corporation on the books of the Treasury Department of the United States.

1870, Dec. 5.
Authority to Treasurer to collect N. Y. interest.

Resolved, That Gouverneur M. Ogden, the Treasurer of this corporation, be authorized to receive from time to time, as it shall accrue, the interest on any stock or evidence of indebtedness of the State of New York, standing in the name of this corporation, and to give the proper receipts and acquittances for the same.

1870, Dec. 19.
Pavement 50th street.

Resolved, That the Treasurer be authorized to take such measures as he may deem necessary to prevent the laying of wooden pavement in 50th street, between 4th and 6th avenues, and to secure the pavement of such street with some approved stone pavement, and to that end to sign on behalf of this corporation any petition or remonstrance to the proper city authorities.

1871, Mar. 6.   *Resolved*, That the Treasurer be authorized to make compensation to the instructors who performed the duties of Professor Egleston during his absence, to an amount not to exceed three hundred dollars.

1871, June 5.
Grant to City Corporation.   *Resolved*, That the Clerk be authorized to execute and affix the corporate seal to a grant and release, in the usual form, to the Mayor, Aldermen, and Commonalty of the City of New York, of the land taken from this corporation by virtue of the proceedings for the extension of Park Place; such grant and release to be delivered upon the payment to Gouverneur M. Ogden, the Treasurer of this corporation, of the award made to this corporation in the same proceeding.

1871, Nov. 6.
Bond to be assigned to Miss. Gelston.   It appearing that Miss Mary I. Gelston, as surety, has paid to the Treasurer the amount secured to be paid by a bond to this corporation, executed by her and Mr. Jeremiah Loder, to secure $2,465.82, bearing date the sixth day of February, 1871: On the application of Miss Gelston, *Resolved*, That such bond be assigned to her, and that the Clerk be authorized to execute and affix the corporate seal to a proper instrument to effect such assignment.

1871, Nov. 6.
Commutation Rhinelander rents.   Likewise *Resolved*, That the Treasurer be authorized to commute the annual rents, amounting in the aggregate to $371.59, renewed by sundry grants in fee of lots lying west of Greenwich street, now belonging to the estate of William Rhinelander, deceased, upon receiving from Mr. Rhinelander's executors the sum of $7,431.80, together with the payment of such rent, *pro rata*, computed to the day of the payment of the said capital sum.

| | TREASURER. | 85 |

1871, Nov. 6.
Treasurer instructed, Gebhard Professor.
  Resolved, That the Treasurer be authorized to pay the Gebhard Professor seventy-two dollars and eighteen cents, being the surplus of the income of the Gebhard Fund for the financial year last past, over the amount allowed to him for salary for the same period.

1872, April 1.
  Resolved, That the Treasurer be authorized, under the direction of the Standing Committee, in order to raise the sum of money necessary to be paid on such a contract, to sell, assign and transfer any stocks or bonds and mortgages belonging to the accumulated fund; and to issue bonds of this Corporation for any part of the purchase money that cannot conveniently be paid in cash; to be secured, if necessary, by mortgage of the land purchased.

  Also, *Resolved*, That the payment of the principal and interest of the mortgages so to be assigned be guarantied on the part of this Corporation; the form of such guarantee to be settled by the Standing Committee.

1872, June 3.
Payment for ball ground for Sophomores and Freshmen.
  Resolved, That the Treasurer be, and he is hereby authorized to advance, as early after the passage of this resolution as may be, such portion of the appropriation for the encouragement of sports and games, made for the ensuing academic year, as may suffice to secure the control, until December next, of the ball ground mentioned in the petition presented to the Trustees to-day, in behalf of the Sophomore and Freshman classes.

1872, Oct. 7.
Dr. Moore's annuity.
  Resolved, That the Treasurer be authorized, in paying to the executor of the late Dr. Nathaniel F. Moore the balance due for the annuity heretofore granted to Dr. Moore by this Board, to compute the same to the day of his death.

1872, Nov. 4.
Power to sell stock.
  Resolved, That Gouverneur M. Ogden, the Treasurer of the Trustees of Columbia College, in the city of New York, have authority to sell, assign, and transfer, from

time to time, as occasion may require, the certificate or certificates of any stock or bonds of the State of New York, standing in the name of this Corporation.

<small>Clerk to furnish copy of the preceding resolution</small> *Resolved,* That the Clerk be authorized to furnish to the Treasurer a certified copy of the last preceding resolution, from time to time, when authorized to do so by the Standing Committee, to which the corporate seal shall be affixed.

<small>1873, June 2. Treasurer to receive awards for land taken.</small> *Resolved,* That Gouverneur M. Ogden, as Treasurer, be authorized to receive the award or awards payable to this Corporation as mortgagees for land taken under proceedings for that purpose, for the laying out a road or public drive, northward from the southerly line of 155th street, in the city of New York, to the intersection of the Kingsbridge road, with a street known and designated on the map of the Department of Public Parks as Inwood street, as laid out by resolution of the Commissioners of the Central Park, and also the award which may be payable to this Corporation as mortgagees for land taken under proceedings for that purpose, for the opening of the Eleventh avenue, from the northerly line of the road or public drive to the southerly line of the street leading from Kingsbridge road, near Inwood street, to the Harlem River, near Sherman's Creek, in the city of New York.

TRUSTEES.

<small>1869, Feb. 1. Meetings called by Chairman.</small> *Resolved,* That in future, when meetings are called by the chairman, upon the requisition of trustees and publication of the same, the papers be entered on the minutes.

MATRICULATION BOOK RECOVERED.

<small>1869, Feb. 1. Thanks to Dr. Francis.</small> *Resolved,* That the thanks of this board be presented to Samuel W. Francis, M. D., for his courtesy in restoring to the college the matriculation book of the medical

department of the college, covering the period from 1791 to 1813, the same having been found among the books of his father, the late Dr. John W. Francis of this city.

<small>1869, Feb. 1.
Prof. Adrain's Portrait.</small>

Resolved, That the president be authorized to permit a copy to be taken of the portrait of the late Professor Adrain, for the use of his son, G. B. Adrain, Esq., and to deliver the picture for the purpose to such artist as the said Mr. G. B. Adrain may select, demanding such guarantees as may seem to him proper to secure the said picture from injury, and to insure its return to the college within a reasonable time.

<small>1869, May 3.
Resignation of Mr. Fish.</small>

Resolved, That this board having duly considered the resignation tendered by Mr. Fish, recently called to the office of Secretary of State of the United States of America, do not deem it unfitting to express their gratification that another incumbent of a high national position has been selected from the rolls of the college.

Resolved, That they are unwilling to accept his resignation, either as trustee or chairman; that they have long enjoyed the advantage of his friendship and his counsel, in both capacities, and are unwilling to relinquish either; that they do not consider the offices now held in the college as incompatible with the full exercise of the new and higher duties which have lately been assigned to him in the councils of the country; that they hope that he will still give to the college such a portion of his time as may be consistent with those duties; and that they cannot consent to sever the tie which has so long bound him and his associates together without a more imperative necessity than now seems to exist.

Resolved, That the chairman be relieved from his duties on the committees of the college.

Resolved, That he be respectfully requested to withdraw his resignation.

Resolved, That a copy of these resolutions, under the seal of the college, and the attestation of the clerk, be transmitted to Mr. Fish.

DONATIONS TO THE LIBRARY.

1869, Dec. 6. Thanks to Rev. Dr. Brown. *Resolved*, That the thanks of the trustees be presented to the Rev. John Brown, D. D., of Newburgh, for his valuable donation to the library of the college, of the Journals of the Convention of the Diocese of New York, from 1805 down nearly to the present time; and that the clerk of the board be requested to communicate to Dr. Brown a copy of this resolution.

1869, Dec. 6. Thanks to Messrs. MacMillan. *Resolved*, That the thanks of the trustees be presented to Messrs. Macmillan & Co., publishers, of London, for their generous contribution to the library of the college of a large number of their valuable publications, amounting to one hundred and thirty-three volumes; and that the clerk of this board be requested to communicate a copy of this resolution to Messrs. Macmillan.

PROPOSED ASSOCIATION WITH COOPER UNION.

The president presented the following preamble and resolution, which were adopted:

1869, Dec. 6. Cooper Union. *Whereas*, It appears from statements before this board that the institution called the Cooper Union may possibly be disposed to associate itself with Columbia College on terms which may be advantageous to both the institutions interested, be it therefore

Committee to confer. *Resolved*, That a committee consisting of five members of this Board be appointed to confer with any similar committee appointed on behalf of the trustees of said Cooper Union, with a view to ascertain whether and upon what terms such an association can be effected; and that they report to the board the result of said conference.

The Rev. Dr. Barnard, Mr. Ogden, Mr. Ruggles, Mr. Nash and Dr. Jay were appointed the committee.

1869, Dec. 20. Death of Mr. Jones.

Resolved, That the members of this Board have heard with great sorrow of the death of their esteemed associate, Edward Jones, Esq., long a Trustee of this College, whose presence among us was as valuable from his intelligence, judgment, and earnest devotion to the welfare of the institution, as it was rendered agreeable by his high character and engaging personal qualities.

Resolved, That a copy of this resolution be transmitted to the family of our departed friend, with an earnest expression of the sympathy of the members of this Board.

1871, May 1. Dr. Torrey's house.

Resolved, That it be permitted to Dr. Torrey, on condition that his services to the college be continued, to reside in the house now occupied by him, on the college grounds, during the pleasure of the Board of Trustees.

1872, Oct. 7. Request to Mr. Rutherfurd to withdraw his resignation.

Resolved, That Mr. Rutherfurd be requested to withdraw his resignation; and that leave of absence be given him for two years.

1873, April 7. Death of Dr. Torrey. Resolutions thereon.

Whereas, It has pleased Him who holds in His hands the destinies of men, to remove from earth our honored and esteemed associate, Dr. John Torrey, for seventeen years a member of this Board, therefore *Resolved,* That while we bow with humble submission to the afflictive dispensation which has thus overtaken us, we feel that this bereavement has deprived us of a colleague whose wisdom in council, whose conscientious fidelity in the discharge of duty, and whose lively interest in the prosperity of our college, will not soon be adequately replaced.

Resolved, That the large and valuable contributions made by our lamented associate to the advancement of science, and especially to his favorite branch of Natural History, have created a monument to his memory more honorable than any which the hands of his surviving friends could erect, and have inscribed his name high in the list of those devoted students of nature whose names have illustrated the scientific progress of the nineteenth century.

Resolved, That the personal character of Dr. Torrey, in which were blended the utmost modesty of self-appreciation with a generous recognition of the merits of others, and an unswerving rectitude of moral principles with the tenderest charity for the faults and weaknesses to which he was himself superior ; and in which it was further shown how respect for the methods of rigorous demonstration, employed in the investigations of modern science, may co-exist and harmonize with the highest reverence for those momentous truths whose source is above the domain of demonstration, and which come by direct revelation from the author of Nature himself, are such as to command the admiration and win the affection of all with whom he came in contact while living, and to form a lasting subject of pleasing recollection, now that he passed away.

Resolved, That we tender our heartfelt sympathies to the surviving members of Dr. Torrey's family, trusting that in the remembrance of his many virtues, and especially of his unaffected piety and uncomplaining resignation under the many trials of life, they may find something to console them in their heavy bereavement.

Resolved, That a copy of these resolutions, properly engrossed, be transmitted to the brother and children of our departed colleague.

1873, April 7. Use of Dr. Torrey's house offered to his daughters.

Resolved, That the Trustees respectfully tender to the daughters of their late esteemed colleague, Dr. Torrey, who are resident on the college grounds, the use of the house now occupied by them, should they be disposed to remain in it, until the first day of May, 1874.

1873, April 7.
Portrait of Dr. Torrey.

Resolved, That a portrait of Dr. Torrey be painted and placed in the Library, under the direction of a Committee to consist of Messrs. Schermerhorn, Swords, Strong, and Nash, and the President.

TUTORSHIPS.

1868, Oct. 5.
Tutor in English Department.

Resolved, That the President be authorized to employ, during the present academic term, some suitable person to discharge the duties of tutor in the English Department, at the salary which is paid at present, or which shall be hereafter fixed as the salary of a tutor in the college.

1869, March 1.
Tutor in English Department.

Resolved, That the President be authorized to appoint some suitable person to discharge the duties of tutor in the English Department, from the beginning of the second academic term during the present year, at the rate of compensation now paid to the officer holding that place.

1869, June 7.
Tutor in English department.

Resolved, That the President be authorized to employ some suitable person to serve as tutor or instructor in English subjects in the college until the close of the first session in the ensuing academic year, at a compensation equal to that which is paid during the same period as the salary of the tutor in Latin and Greek.

1872, June 3.
Tutorship in Rhetoric.

Resolved, That in the case the tutorship in Rhetoric and History shall fall vacant after the adjournment of this meeting of the Trustees, and that said tutorship be not discontinued by any action taken during this meeting, the President be authorized to appoint some suitable person to discharge the duties of such tutorship at the established rate of compensation, provided that the person so appointed be nominated to the Trustees at the stated meeting in October next for confirmation.

SCHOOL OF MINES.

FEES.

1873, June 3.

Resolved, further, That the Treasurer be authorized to return to their signers any notes which may be now in his possession heretofore given under the liberty of option allowed by the clause repealed in the foregoing resolution, taking their several receipts for the same; and that the said obligations be no longer counted as among the assets of the college.

FOREIGN EXCHANGE.

1868, May 4.
Foreign exch'nge

Resolved, That an appropriation be made, not exceeding one thousand dollars, from the contingent fund of the School of Mines, for the financial year commencing on the first day of October, 1868, for the purpose of continuing the system of exchanges of minerals and scientific publications which has been commenced with foreign school.

1869, Nov. 1.
Foreign exchanges.

Resolved, That the sum of eleven hundred dollars be appropriated to the purpose of continuing, for the current year, the system of exchanges with foreign institutions, on the part of the School of Mines, to be expended, as heretofore, under the direction of the president.

1872, March 2.

Resolved, That for the future the Professor of Mineralogy and Metallurgy shall acquire, by purchase or exchange, for the collections under his charge, only such specimens as may be applicable to and necessary for the instruction of the students.

1872, Nov. 4.
Foreign exchanges.

Resolved, That a sum not exceeding three hundred dollars be appropriated to meet any claims that may be outstanding against the college on account of the system of foreign exchanges heretofore in operation, and to close up the business of said system of foreign exchanges, by forwarding publications already collected for transmission to European institutions, and minerals, in return for collections received from abroad, for which suitable returns have not yet been made.

ADMISSION.

1868, Jan. 1. Admission to Preparatory Class S. of M.

Resolved, That candidates for admission to the preparatory department of the School of Mines may be received on passing satisfactorily the required examinations, provided they shall have completed their seventeenth year.

FREE TUITION.

1868, Nov. 2. Privilege to Students in S. of M.

Resolved, That hereafter any student of the School of Mines who shall have been for three years a member of the school, pursuing any one of the regular courses of instruction, and shall have fully paid up all his fees and other liabilities to the school, may, with the consent of the president, continue his attendance and enjoy the privileges of the school without any charge for tuition.

1873, June 3. Notes of Students.

Resolved, That the resolution of the Trustees adopted April 3, 1865, as to the college, and extended by resolution of October 9, 1865, so as to be applicable to the School of Mines, providing that under certain conditions a student may receive instruction free of charge for tuition, with the clause annexed: That, " in case he," the said student, " shall so elect, he may give his note for the amount to be paid at his convenience after graduation," be, and the same hereby is, repealed as to the said annexed clause above cited, the body of the resolution remaining still valid.

SCHOLARSHIPS.

1872, June 3.
Notice of motion to Amend Statute of School of Mines.
The President gave notice of a motion "to amend the amendment to the statute on the School of Mines, which provides for the creation of free Scholarships in said college, by annexing the following proviso : 'Provided that no such scholarship shall be held by any student in said school unless such student be a member of one of the regular classes of the preparatory class.'"

SALARIES.

1873, Nov. 3.
Resolved, That the provisions of the resolution of January 6th, 1868, granting a temporary increase of twenty-five per cent. on the salaries of the Professors in the School of Mines be likewise continued in force from the fifteenth of November, 1873, until the further order of this Board.

AUTHORITY TO RAISE FUNDS.

1869, April 5.
Donations requested.
Resolved, That the Committee on the School of Mines are hereby authorized to request donations from the alumni, or other friends of the college, of funds for increasing its collections or its library.

SMITHSONIAN MINERALS.

1869, Nov. 9.
Smithsonian Minerals.
Resolved, That the sum of fifty dollars be appropriated, to be expended under the direction of the president, for continuing, during the present year, the examination and arrangement of the Smithsonian minerals, in accordance with the agreement heretofore made with that institution.

1872, Mar. 2.
Resolved, That after the present year the receipt for classification and arrangement of minerals of the Smithsonian Institute, and the appropriation for foreign exchanges, shall be discontinued.

GEOLOGICAL COLLECTION.

1869, Dec. 6.
Insurance of Geology and Paleontology collection.

Resolved, That the communication of Dr. Newberry made to the board, through the president, requesting that the insurance on his collection in Geology and Paleontology be increased, be referred to the Committee on the School of Mines, with power.

1870, May 2.
Dr. Newberry Collection.

Resolved, That it be referred to the Committee on the School of Mines to inquire whether it is desirable that any measure be taken by the Trustees with a view of acquiring possession of the geological and paleontological collection belonging to Dr. Newberry, now on deposit in the School of Mines, and if so, what, and that said Committee report to the Trustees at their regular meeting in October next.

1870, Nov. 7.

Resolution reported by committee :

Resolved, That the Board consent to the proposition made by Dr. Newberry, to transfer to them the possession of his entire Geological and Paleontological Collection with such additions as he may hereafter be able to make to it, for the sum of fifteen thousand dollars, the same to be paid to him in instalments as follows : three thousand dollars on the   day of   and the remainder in instalments, to be paid severally on the   day of   in each succeeding year until the whole is paid ; and to bear interest in the meantime from and after the   day of   .

Dr. Newberry's collection.

The report was accepted and the recommendation accompanying the same adopted, except that it was ordered that three thousand dollars be paid in cash and the residue with interest within the year at the pleasure of the board. Laid over for action under the ordinance.

1870, Dec. 19.
Second reading of purchase of Dr. Newberry's collection.

The action of the Trustees taken on the seventh of November last, directing the purchase of Dr. Newberry's collection, was again considered under the ordinance establishing the financial policy of the college, was again considered and affirmed.

LABORATORIES.

1873, Jan. 6. Blowpipe Laboratory, referred to Standing Committee. — *Resolved,* That the Standing Committee be instructed to inquire and report what measures ought to be taken, if any, to enlarge the Blowpipe Laboratory of the School of Mines.

$150 appropriated for tables for Prof. Egleston. — *Resolved,* That one hundred and fifty dollars be appropriated to complete the payment for the construction of working tables in the Laboratory of Prof. Egleston, in addition to the sum ($150) heretofore appropriated for the same purpose.

ASSISTANTS.

1870, Dec. 5. Assistant in College and School of Mines. — *Resolved,* That hereafter no assistant paid from the general funds of the college shall be employed in any department of the College or School of Mines, except under appointment of the Board of Trustees, and that no person shall hold a place as assistant as aforesaid who is at the same time an undergraduate student in said College or School of Mines; but this resolution shall not apply to any assistant now employed.

1872, Dec. 2. Honorary assistants in the School of Mines. — *Resolved,* That the President be authorized to employ as honorary assistants, without compensation, in those departments of the School of Mines in which such assistants can be of use, graduates of said school, or proficients in science elsewhere educated, whom he may deem competent to the duties they are expected to perform; provided the candidates for such appointments shall be recommended by the Professors in the departments in which they are to be employed.

STUDENTS.

1870, April 4.
$25 to be paid to Mr. A. Barnard.

Resolved, That the sum of $25 be paid to Mr. Alfred Barnard as a reward for returning to the College a piece of platinum which had been stolen.

1871, Nov. 6
Application Sch. Hamilton granted.

An application of Schuyler Hamilton, to be allowed to attend a course of instruction in drawing in the School of Mines, was granted.

1872, Nov. 4.
Leave to J. Aymar to take drawing lessons.

Resolved, That Mr. José Aymar be permitted to take lessons in Drawing in the School of Mines, provided such arrangements can be made for the purpose as to prevent any interruption to his proper duties in the college.

1873, Jan. 6.
Leave to Messrs Buckley and Storrs to take drawing lessons.

Resolved, That Mr. C. R. Buckley and Mr. Frank Storrs be permitted to take lessons in drawing in the School of Mines during the pleasure of the President, provided such lessons do not interfere with their studies in college, and that arrangements can be conveniently made for them by the Professor of Drawing.

PRINTING.

1871, Feb. 6.
Article on Mining Education to be printed.

Resolved, That fifteen hundred copies of the article on "Mining Education," published in the *North American Review* for January, with a suitable introduction by the President of the College, be printed for general circulation, the cost of the same to be defrayed out of the appropriation already made for printing for School of Mines, provided that the work can be done at an expense not exceeding ninety dollars.

PURCHASE OF METEORITES.

1873, Jan. 6.
Application of Prof. Egleston for $100 declined.

Resolved, That the application of Prof. Egleston for an appropriation of one hundred dollars for the purchase of certain meteorites be declined.

SUSPENSION OF EXERCISES.

1872, Dec. 2.
Suspension of exercises School of Mines.

Resolved, That it has not been the intention of the Trustees in any resolution or resolutions now in force, to authorize the suspension of exercises in the School of Mines during the period devoted to the intermediate examination in the college, or to preparation for the same; and that hereafter no interruption of the exercises shall take place in the school during said period, except in the departments filled by Professors whose duties require them to be engaged at that time in the examinations of the college.

BY-LAWS.

1872, June 3.
By-Laws of School of Mines, age of admission.

Resolved, That the by-laws of the School of Mines be amended in Section 1 and Section 10, relating to the age, limiting admission to the regular and preparatory classes of the School, by adding in Section 1, after the words "eighteen years of age," the following words, being a transcript of the provision of the statute regulating admission to the college, Chap. IV., § 1, "but this rule may be dispensed with when, in the opinion of the Faculty, there are sufficient reasons for the relaxation;" and also by adding, in Section 10, the same words after the words "seventeen years of age," a period being placed at the end of the addition; and the succeeding words being so altered as in place of "and must" to read "They must."

INSTRUCTION IN FRENCH AND GERMAN.

1870, Mar. 7.
Instruction in French and German.

Resolved, That the Committee on the School of Mines be authorized to recommend some properly qualified person or persons to give instruction in the French language to the students of the School of Mines, the said instructor being expected to enter upon his duties on the first Monday in October next; to give if required eight lessons per week to classes in said School throughout the scholastic year, and to receive compensation at the rate of one thousand dollars a year for such service.

Resolved further, That if the Board of Trustees shall see fit to authorize or require instruction in French to be given to undergraduate students, then the same instructor may be employed to give, if required, four lessons per week throughout the scholastic year to undergraduate classes, regular or voluntary, and that in case the amount of service rendered by him be so increased, his compensation shall be also increased to twelve hundred dollars per annum.

Resolved, That the Committee inquire whether or not such an arrangement can be made of the exercises in the undergraduate department as to make it possible for the Gebhard Professor, with his own consent, to give instruction in the German language in the School of Mines, eight lessons per week to be given to classes in said School throughout the scholastic year, and that in the event such arrangement shall be found practicable, the Gebhard Professor shall give such instruction; but that in case of the failure of this provision the Committee shall have power to recommend some other suitably qualified person or persons to perform said service, to enter upon his duties on the first Monday in October next, and to be compensated at the rate of one thousand dollars per annum.

DEGREES.

1871, Mar 6. Degree of Ph. D. referred to Committee. School of Mines.

Resolved, That it be referred to the Committee on the School of Mines to report, 1st: Whether it is expedient that the Degree of Doctor in Philosophy be conferred in course; and 2d. In case it should be thought expedient, what qualifications ought to be required of candidates as the condition of granting such degree.

1873, April 7. Ph.D. referred to Committee on School of Mines.

Resolved, That the Committee on the School of Mines be instructed to inquire and report to this Board whether the time has not arrived at which it is expedient to prescribe a supplementary course of instruction in science, leading to the degree of Doctor of Philosophy in the School of Mines; and if so, to prepare and present to the Board an outline of such course for their consideration.

1873, May 5.
Degree of Ph.D.

Resolved, That the degree of Doctor of Philosophy be conferred upon any graduate of the School of Mines who shall have pursued for an academic year at the School a systematic course of higher study under the direction of the Faculty in two or more branches of science, and shall have been examined thereon, and who shall have presented an acceptable thesis or dissertation embodying the results of such special study and observation.

1875, June 3.
Ph.D.

Resolved, That the degree of Doctor of Philosophy be conferred upon any graduate of the School of Mines who shall have pursued, for one academic year, a systematic course of higher study, under the direction of the Faculty, in two or more branches of study, and shall have been examined thereon, and who shall have presented an acceptable thesis or dissertation embodying the results of such special study and observation.

DONATIONS.

1868, May 4.
Russian Government.

Resolved, That a letter be addressed by the chairman of the board to the Russian Government, expressing the thanks of this board for the liberal donation of minerals made to the School of Mines.

1869, Dec. 6.
Thanks to W. A. Smith, E. M.

Resolved, That the thanks of the Trustees be presented to W. A. Smith, E. M., a graduate of the School of Mines, for the valuable collection of specimens presented by him to the school, illustrating the manufacture of Bessemer steel at Twickhan, in Germany.

1869, Dec. 6.
Thanks to Messrs. Parrott and Aspinwall.

Resolved, That the thanks of the Trustees be presented to Robert P. Parrott, Esq., and to W. H. Aspinwall, Esq., for their generous contributions towards purchasing the valuable collections of minerals made by Prof. Egleston, in Europe, during the past summer, with a view to making them a donation to the cabinet of mineralogy in the School of Mines.

1870, Feb. 7.
Thanks to M. K. Jessup.

Resolved, That the thanks of the Trustees be presented to Morris K. Jessup, Esq., for his liberal donation to the Department of Mineralogy in the School of Mines, and that the Clerk of the Board be requested to transmit to Mr. Jessup a copy of this resolution.

1870, Feb. 7.
G. Kemble.

Resolved, That the thanks of the Trustees be presented to Gouverneur Kemble, Esq., for his liberal donation to the Department of Mineralogy in the School of Mines, and that the Clerk of the Board be requested to transmit to Mr. Kemble a copy of this resolution.

1870, Feb. 7.
D. S. Egleston.

Resolved, That the thanks of the Trustees be presented to D. S. Egleston, Esq., for his liberal donation to the Department of Mineralogy in the School of Mines, and that the Clerk of the Board be requested to transmit to Mr. Egleston a copy of this resolution.

1870, Feb. 7.
W. E. Dodge, Jr.

Resolved, That the thanks of the Trustees be presented to Wm. E. Dodge, Jr., Esq., for his liberal donation to the Department of Mineralogy in the School of Mines, and that the Clerk of the Board be requested to transmit to Mr. Dodge a copy of this resolution.

1870, Feb. 7.
Messrs. M. K. Jessup & Co.

Resolved, That the thanks of the Trustees be presented to Messrs. M. K. Jessup & Co., for their liberal donation to the Department of Mineralogy in the School of Mines, and that the Clerk of the Board be requested to transmit to Messrs. M. K. Jessup & Co. a copy of this resolution.

1870, Apr. 4.
Thanks to Dr. Agnew.

Resolved, That the thanks of the Trustees be presented to Dr. C. R. Agnew for his contribution towards the purchase of optical apparatus for the determination of the crystalline character of minerals, and that a copy of this resolution be communicated to Dr. Agnew by the Clerk of the Board.

1870, Apr. 4.
Thanks to Mr. Lanier.

Resolved, That the thanks of the Trustees be presented to Charles Lanier, Esq., for the interesting and valuable collection of crystals of gold presented by him to the Mineralogical Cabinet of the School of Mines, and that a copy of this resolution be communicated to Mr. Lanier by the Clerk of the Board.

1873, June 3.

Whereas, it has been communicated to this Board that Mrs. R. L. Allen, of Saratoga Springs, has presented to the College the collection of minerals of her late husband, Dr. R. L. Allen, at his request,

Thanks to Mrs. R. L. Allen.

Resolved, That the President be authorized to make to Mrs. Allen a suitable acknowledgment of this gift, in the name of the Trustees.

LAW SCHOOL.

1868, May 4.
Annual Sermon at Law School.

The chairman of the Committee on the Law School reported that the annual sermon would be delivered by the Reverend Philander K. Cady, at Trinity Church, and asked that one hundred dollars be appropriated for the necessary expenses attending the delivery of the sermon. The appropriation was made.

1868, June 1.
Stated meeting.

Ordered, that the Committee on the Law School shall hereafter hold a stated meeting at the Law School, on the third Saturday of January, at half-past three P. M. Also,

1868, Dec. 7.
Accommodation for Law School.

Resolved, That the board be requested to authorize this committee to take such steps as may be necessary to secure accommodations for the Law School for such period as may be expedient.

LAW SCHOOL. 103

1869, May, 3.
Duplicate law diplomas.

Resolved, That a duplicate copy of the diploma be given by the Warden of the Law School to such graduates as are residents of the Second Judicial District of the State, at any time after the time of passing due examination, with the view of furnishing to them such evidence as to enable them to obtain admission to the bar in that district at the ensuing General Term of the Supreme Court therein.

The minutes of the Committee on the School of Mines of April 6, 1869, were read, which contained the following resolutions ·

1869, June 7.
Addresses at Law School Commencement.

Resolved, That 500 copies of the addresses at the recent commencement of the Law School, delivered by the warden of the school, by General Tremaine from the Alumni, and by Henry Nicoll, Esq., be published together under the direction of the warden of the school.

1870, Feb. 7.
Law School Committee to provide accommodations.

Resolved, That the Law Committee have authority to hire the building now occupied as a Law School, or some other appropriate premises.

1870, June 6.
Thanks to Messrs. Roelker, Curtis and Wetmore.

Resolved, That the thanks of the Board be and they are hereby presented to Messrs. Bernard Roelker, William E. Curtis, and Edward Wetmore, for their services as Examiners of the papers submitted by members of the graduating class of 1870, competing for the prize in the department of Political Science and Public Law, and that the Clerk furnish a copy of this resolution to those gentlemen respectively.

1870, June 6.
Thanks to Messrs. Strong, Parsons and Wright.

Resolved, That the thanks of the Board be and they are hereby presented to the Honorable Theron R. Strong, and to Messrs. John E. Parsons and George W. Wright for their services as Examiners of the papers submitted by members of the graduating class of 1870, competing for the prize in the department of Municipal Law, and that the Clerk furnish a copy of this resolution to those gentlemen respectively.

LAW SCHOOL.

1870, June 6.
Thanks to Dr. Morgan.
Resolved, That the thanks of the Board be presented to the Rev. William F. Morgan, D. D., for his sermon preached before the graduating class of the Law School on the evening of May 15, 1870, and that he be respectfully requested to furnish a copy of the same for publication.

1871, Feb. 6.
Warden to regulate the election of Valedictorian.
Resolved, That the Warden of the Law School shall have power to prescribe the mode which the members of the Senior Class in the School shall pursue in the election of the Valedictorian.

1872, June 3.
Rev. Dr. Potter's Sermon.
Resolved, That the Chairman of the Law School Committee request from Rev. Henry Potter, D. D., a copy, for publication, of his sermon preached before the graduating class of the Law School of 1871.

Bishop Potter's Sermon.
Resolved, That the thanks of the Trustees be returned to the Right Rev. Horatio Potter, D. D., D. C. L., for the sermon preached by him before the graduating class of the Law School on Sunday evening, May 12th, 1872; and that he be requested to furnish a copy thereof for publication; and that a copy of this resolution be sent to him by the Clerk of this Board.

1872, Oct. 7.
Memorial of Prof. Lieber, referred to Committee on Law School.
Resolved, That it be referred to the Law School Committee to prepare and report to the Board at the next stated meeting a suitable minute in memory of Francis Lieber, late Professor of Constitutional History and Public Law in the College Law School.

1872, Nov. 4.
Mr. Bidwell.
Resolved, That in the death of Marshall L. Bidwell, LL.D., one of the Lecturers in the Law School, the legal profession and society at large have sustained a severe loss. Mr. Bidwell was a thorough and accurate lawyer, comprehensive in knowledge, being equally familiar with great principles and minute details, clear in argument, and eminently sound and practical in judgment. He was a safe counsellor, and worthy of absolute confidence as a man of spotless integrity, and of genuine Christian faith

and practice. He was cheerful and kind in his disposition, eager to impart his varied information to those who sought it, and strong in his desire to promote the good of society. He was a steadfast and earnest friend of the Law School, hoping that it might aid in the advancement of legal education. To the memory of the man so learned, so kind-hearted, so true and so wise, the Board pays this simple tribute, knowing how far short it falls of an adequate expression of his solid attainments and moral worth.

Resolved, That a copy of the foregoing resolution be sent to the family of deceased.

<small>1872, Nov. 4.
Building and maintenance of Law School.</small>

Resolved, That the Committee on the Law School inquire and report whether a building larger than that now occupied by it can be hired, and upon what terms.

<small>Referred to the Law Committee.</small>

Resolved, That the same Committee consider and report whether any alterations ought to be made in the regulations for the support of the Law School, whereby it is provided that the rent shall be paid by the college.

<small>1873, Feb. 3.
Dr. Lieber.</small>

Resolved, That the Law School has met with a serious loss in the death of Francis Lieber, LL.D., Professor of Constitutional History and Public Law. While the topics upon which he lectured lie beyond the ordinary course of legal instruction, they are considered by this Board to be of grave importance as lifting the student beyond the range of technical law to a wide field of vision and research. To the great themes of Political Science and Constitutional Law, Dr. Lieber performed thoughtfulness of illustration and earnestness of exposition, and left, as we believe, on the minds of students who carefully followed his teachings, lasting and most valuable impressions. It should be added that Dr. Lieber's studies have not been confined to the duties of the class-room, and that some of the most important of his published works, received by leading jurists with marked favor, have been produced during his connection with this college as one of its Professors.

Resolved, That the Board records with satisfaction Dr. Lieber's steadfast adherence to the great principles of Christianity, not only as the basis of his political views, but as a rule of individual life. While he gladly recognized throughout the civilized world the general growth of Nationalism, he had full faith in the brotherhood of man and in his sublime destiny.

Personally, he was an earnest patriot. In youth he was ready to shed his blood in defence of his native land; in his old age he rendered efficient service with his pen and voice to his adopted country during its late struggle. He was a man of sterling integrity, clear and decided in his opinions, and bold and outspoken in their advocacy. His excellencies were so great and manifold as to justify the statement that a great thinker, a genuine Christian, a true patriot, and an estimable citizen in all the relations of private life, has departed, and has left a name long to be remembered and valued in connection with Columbia College and its Law School.

Wherever his works are read, and his character is known, it will be felt that the principles of Christianity, which lie at the root of the history and discipline of the college, are well illustrated by his life and labors.

Resolved, That a copy of the foregoing resolutions be sent to the family of Dr. Lieber.

1873, April 7.
Warden to have charge of the new Law School.

Resolved, That the care of the Law School building, No. 8 Great Jones street, shall appertain to the Warden of the Law School, who shall have power to make needful rules and regulations concerning its management and the duties of the Janitor, subject from time to time to revision by the Law Committee.

LAW SCHOOL.

INSTRUCTION.

1868, June 1. Assistant Professor in Law School. I. There shall be for the academic year 1868–9, an assistant professor in the department of municipal law, whose duty it shall be to give instruction in such branches of municipal law as may be assigned to him by the warden, with the concurrence of the Committee on the Law School.

Compensation. II. The compensation of such Assistant Professor shall be   to be paid from the general funds of the college.

1871, June 5. Law School, third year. *Resolved*, That it be referred to the Committee on the Law School, with power to add a third or additional year to the present course of the School, and, if they deem it expedient, to establish regulations and prescribe the course of study for such additional year, it being understood that all attendance on such third year is not to be required to obtain the degree of Bachelor of Laws.

Adjunct Professor Law School. *Resolved*, That the Law School Committee be authorized to appoint an Adjunct Professor of Municipal Law, for such term of office as to it shall seem expedient, to perform such duties in instruction as may be assigned to him by the committee; his compensation not to exceed three thousand dollars per annum; and to be paid as provided by the resolution of the Board passed February 1st, 1864.

1871, Oct. 2. Mr. Austin Abbott, Adjunct Professor of Municipal Law. Mr. Ruggles reported that the Law Committee had appointed Mr. Austin Abbott Adjunct Professor of Municipal Law, to hold his office for one year from the 15th August, 1871, at a compensation of three thousand dollars for the year.

1872, Dec. 2. Instruction in Dr. Lieber's department, referred to Law Committee. *Resolved*, That the Law Committee be instructed to consider the expediency of temporarily providing for one or more courses of instruction on the topics embraced in Dr. Lieber's department; with power to make such provision. Also, *Resolved*, That the Committee report at the next meeting of the Board their action on this subject.

1873, Jan. 6.   *Resolved*, That it is expedient to make temporary provision for one or more courses of instruction in the topics embraced in Dr. Lieber's department.

1873, Jan. 6.   *Resolved*, That Prof. Dwight be requested to invite the Rev. Elisha Mulford, of Friendship, Pa., to deliver during the present academic year a course of lectures on Political Science, and Mr. Geo. H. Yeaman to deliver during the same period a course of lectures on Constitutional Law; and Mr. Charles McLean a course on Private International Law, or on Civil Law; the compensation of these gentlemen to be at the rate of fifty dollars for each lecture; and the Rev. Mr. Mulford to be repaid his travelling expenses, should any be incurred by him.

And that it be referred to Prof. Dwight to arrange with these gentlemen, in case of their acceptance, as to the number of such lectures and the times of their delivery.

1873, Apr. 7. LL.B to be conferred.   *Resolved*, That the degree of Bachelor of Laws be conferred upon such members of the graduating class as shall be recommended by the Law Committee after the ensuing examination.

Dr. Lieber's professorship.   *Resolved*, That the Law Committee of the Trustees be instructed to inquire what changes, if any, should be made in the title of the chair lately rendered vacant by the death of Dr. Lieber, and what subject should be assigned to that department, and what other professorships or lectureships should be established, and that such Committee report, if practicable, at the next meeting of the Board.

Resolved, That the Clerk furnish a copy of the foregoing resolution to the Warden of the Law School.

LAW SCHOOL. 109

1873, May 5.
Instruction in the Law School.
Resolved, That Mr. Geo. H. Yeaman, Mr. McLean, and Professor Burgess, now residing in Berlin, Germany, be invited to deliver courses of lectures for the ensuing year in the Law School, on the topics now appertaining mainly to the department of the late Dr. Lieber. Each course shall contain sixteen lectures or thereabouts, the precise number to be decided upon on consultation with the Warden. The topics for the course of Professor Burgess shall be Political Science; that for the course of Mr. Yeaman, Constitutional Law; and the subject of Mr. McLean's course shall be International Law, Public and Private. The gentlemen named will consult with the Warden as to the times which will be most useful to the students and which are not considered in his own course of lectures.

Compensation.
Resolved, That the compensation for the respective courses to be paid to each lecturer shall be one thousand dollars.

Faculty in Law School.
Resolved, That the Committee on the Law School take into consideration and report, at as early a day as possible, on the propriety of establishing a Faculty of the Law School.

EXPENDITURES.

1871, Feb. 6.
$250 appropriated to ventilation.
Resolved, That two hundred and fifty dollars be appropriated for the ventilation of rooms in the Law School.

1872, Nov. 4.
Bill of six hundred and eight dollars and twenty-nine cents for repairs in Law School.
On the like recommendation it was ordered that a bill of William Wilson & Son, of six hundred and eight dollars and twenty-nine cents, for repairs to the Law School, be paid.

1873, Jan. 6.
Mr. Randolph's fee to be refunded.
Resolved, On the recommendation of the Committee on the Law School that the Treasurer be authorized to refund to Mr. Hector C. F. Randolph his fee as a law student for the present year, amounting to one hundred dollars.

LAW SCHOOL.

1873, Feb. 3. Upon the recommendation of the Committee on the Law School.

$300 appropriation for Law School Commencement. *Resolved*, That the appropriation for the expenses of the Commencement of the Law School be increased to three hundred dollars.

1873, Mar. 3. *Resolved*, That the Clerk be authorized to execute and
Lease of Mr. Schermerhorn's housef or Law School. affix the corporate seal to a lease, between the college as lessee, and Wm. C. Schermerhorn as lessor, by which would be demised, by the latter to the college, the premises at the northwest corner of Lafayette place and Great Jones street, for the term of five years from the first day of May, 1872, at the annual rent for the first three years of $6,000 per annum, and for the remaining two years of $7,000 per annum, with an addition for each year of ten per cent. upon the cost of the alterations necessary to fit the building for the use of the Law School, with such other provisions to be inserted as may be approved by the Clerk and the Treasurer.

1873, April 7. *Resolved*, That the sum of three hundred dollars be
$300 appropriated for removal of Law School. appropriated to pay the expenses of the removal of the Law School to No. 8 Great Jones street, and to procure needful furniture, the said amount to be paid by the Treasurer to the Warden.

1873, June 2. *Resolved*, That the Treasurer be authorized to pay the
Rent of Law School for May. rent of the building No. 37 Lafayette place for the month of May last, at the rate of $3,000 per annum, the same having been occupied during such month by the Law School.

PRIZES.

1868, June 1. *Resolved*, That in view of the small number of students
Prizes in Departments of Constitutional History and Public Law. who attend the lectures in the Department of Constitutional History and Public Law, the prize of two hundred dollars in that department be discontinued after the class of 1869, in the Law School, shall have graduated.

LAW SCHOOL. 111

1868, Dec. 7.
Prizes in Law School.

Resolved, That in view of the fact that the prize in the department of Constitutional History and Public Law was among those announced in the last catalogue, the prize in that department be continued to the present junior class.

1871, April 3.
Report Law Committee to extend prize in Department Public Law, &c., another year.

Mr. Ruggles reported verbally, on behalf of the Law Committee, that the Committee recommend that the prize of two hundred dollars be continued for the present year in the department of "Constitutional History" and "Public Law," and that the committee may, should they deem it expedient, divide the same in such proportions as may be proper.

With power to extend it to 2d year.

They likewise recommend that the committee have power to continue the above prize for the second year, should they deem it expedient to do so, with the same discretion as to dividing it. The recommendations of the committee were adopted.

1872, June 3.
Thanks to the Committee on Prizes in Law School.

Whereas, John M. Knox, Esq., Henry Day, Esq., and John A. Weeks, Esq., were heretofore appointed a committee to award the prize in the department of Municipal Law, and acted as such committee; and *whereas,* the Honorable Charles A. Peabody, Joseph B. Vanum, Esq., and Gilbert H. Crawford, Esq., were heretofore appointed a committee to award the prize in the department of Political Science, and acted as such committee; therefore,

Resolved, That the thanks of this Board be returned to those gentlemen respectively for their valuable services; and that the same be communicated to them by the Clerk of this Board.

Resolved, That the prize in Prof. Lieber's department be continued for another year.

DEGREES.

1870, June 6.
Degree of B. A.

Resolved, That the Board of the College be requested to make hereafter to this Board no recommendations of candidates for the degree of Bachelor of Arts unless said candidate shall have fulfilled all the conditions prescribed by the Statutes for the attainment of said degree.

1872, May 6.
Degree of LL. B.

Resolved, That the President of the College be authorized to confer, at or before the ensuing commencement of the Law School, the degree of Bachelor of Laws upon such members of the graduating class as shall be recommended by the Law Committee, after due examination.

SCHOOL OF MEDICINE.

1873, Nov. 3.
Committee on College of Physicians and Surgeons.

Resolved, That a Committee of five members be appointed to inquire into the relations of the College of Physicians and Surgeons with this college, and to report to this Board.

ORDINANCE ESTABLISHING A PERMANENT FINANCIAL POLICY.

The ordinance of Nov. 26, 1866, establishing a permanent financial policy, having since its adoption been repeatedly amended, it is here reprinted with the several amendments introduced in their proper places.

1866, Nov. 26. *Whereas*, In view of the propriety of extinguishing as early as possible the present indebtedness of the college, of meeting probable assessments for city improvements, and of providing for the college and its schools, buildings more convenient than those occupied by them at present, and better adapted to promote their educational objects, it is expedient that the annual expenditures be kept within such reasonable limits as, while insuring a liberal support to the departments and schools of instruction at present existing, shall leave a surplus for the accumulation of a fund to be applied to the important objects above mentioned; therefore be it ordained, by the trustees of Columbia college, as follows:

ARTICLE I.—The surplus income of the college, which shall remain after the payment of the annual expenditures, shall be annually appropriated and set apart for an accumulating and sinking fund. The said annual expenditures shall only be made for the several purposes hereinafter set forth, and shall not exceed the sums hereinafter named for such purposes. *Provided*, That this rule shall not apply to salaries, nor prevent the creation of any new professorship or other office which the interests of the college may demand; nor prevent the expenditure of the proceeds of sale of any real estate in the acquisition or improvement of any other real estate or buildings in their place.

EXPENDITURES FOR THE ACADEMIC DEPARTMENT.

Departments of instruction:
- Of physics $700
- " chemistry 500
- " mechanics and astronomy 700
- " geodesy and surveying 500
- Botanical collection 700
- Library 3,000
- Classical, English, and mathematical departments 500
- Physical exercises of students * 1500

As to each of these items, if the appropriation made in any year be not expended, in whole or in part, the balance unexpended may be added to the appropriation of the succeeding year.

Prizes	$150
College societies	700
Supplies	3,700
Printing and advertising	2,500
Commencement and exhibitions	500
Scholarships and fellowships	5,500
Contingencies	5,000
Insurance, whatever may be necessary	
Repairs, whatever may be necessary	

TREASURER'S OFFICE.

Expenses of office 250

CLERK'S OFFICE.

Expenses of office 150

---

* Amendment of Dec. 2, 1872.

EXPENDITURES FOR THE SCHOOL OF MINES.

Departments of instruction:
- Of mineralogy.......... $750
- " geology............ 750
- " paleontology *....... 750
- " metallurgy.......... 750
- " metallurgic laboratory 500
- " analytic chemistry.... 4,000
- " applied chemistry†.... 750
- " mining engineering... 750
- " drawing............ 500
- " civil engineering...... 750
- Library................ 2,000

As to each of these items, if the appropriation made in any year be not expended, in whole or in part, the balance unexpended may be added to the appropriation of the succeeding year.

Supplies	$3,500
Foreign exchanges‡	2,000
Printing and advertising	2,500
Repairs, enlargement, alteration, and improvement of building, furniture, and fixtures, whatever may be necessary	
Contingencies	1,500
Prizes	700

EXPENDITURES FOR THE SCHOOL OF LAW.

Rent, whatever may be necessary.

Library	1,000
Supplies	1,500
Prizes	700
Commencement	250
Printing and advertising	750
Repairs, whatever may be necessary.	
Contingencies	1,000

---

* Amendment of May 4, 1867.   † Amendment of June 5, 1871.
‡ Amendment of Oct. 5, 1868.

MISCELLANEOUS EXPENDITURES.

Real estate, whatever may be necessary.
Interest, whatever may be necessary.
Taxes, whatever may be necessary.

Furniture for the president's house.......$250 } If the appropriation in any year be not expended, the balance unexpended may be added to the appropriation of the succeeding year.

Provided, however, That nothing herein contained shall be taken to effect the regulations for the support of the law school heretofore adopted.

ARTICLE II.—Said surplus shall be invested and accumulated, under the direction of the treasurer, the chairman of the board of trustees, and the president of the college, in the name of the college, on bond and mortgage on improved and unincumbered real estate in the city of New York, or in stocks of the United States, or of the State of New York, or of the city of New York; and all interest received thereon, from time to time, shall be so invested. But such surplus or interest may be temporarily invested, under their direction, by deposit in the New York life insurance and trust company or the United States trust company, or by temporary loan to the United States, or in the United Stares treasury notes or certificates of indebtedness.

ARTICLE III.—The said officers above named shall be styled managers of the accumulating fund. They shall keep minutes of their proceedings; and they shall report the same at every meeting of the board of trustees, and shall annually report the condition and amount of said fund, its modes of investment and other matters connected therewith.

ARTICLE IV.—The said fund may be applied from time to time, under the direction of the board of trustees, to the payment of the debt of the college, or of assessments upon its estate imposed by law; or to defray other charges upon its estate, or the cost of the erection of buildings or acquisition of land; but shall be applied to no other purpose until such fund shall amount to five hundred thousand dollars.

ARTICLE V.—This ordinance shall not be altered, amended, or repealed, nor shall any appropriation be made in contravention thereof, without a vote of a majority of the members present, nor unless the proposed alteration, amendment, repeal, or appropriation shall have been presented at a previous meeting, and approved by a majority of the members present at such previous meeting.

ARTICLE VI.—This ordinance shall take effect from and after the first Tuesday of March, 1867.

ERRATA.

The following errors of dates have been found in the Compendium of Resolutions of the Trustees from 1820 to 1868, heretofore printed:

Page 16. 4th marginal date, for 1855, April 5, read 1855, April 2.
" 17. 1st   "   " 1857, Feb. 6, read 1854, Feb. 6.
" 24. 2d   "   " 1851, June 14, read 1861, June 24. Also
In the text, same, "   " June 14, 1851, read June 24, 1861.
Page 25. 4th   "   " 1852, May 2, read 1825, May 2.
" 28. 3d   "   " 1833, May 3, read 1833, May 1.
" 28. 4th   "   " 1839, ———, read 1839, June 3.
" 28. 5th   "   " 1851, June 2, read 1851, May 5.
" 30. 2d   "   " 1851, June 15, read 1857, June 15, and
Also in text, same, "   " ———, June 15, read June 15, 1857.
Page 39. 3d   "   " 1831, Dec. 5, read 1831, Jan. 4.
Also in text, same, "   " December, 1831, read January, 1831.
Page 42. 3d   "   " 1858, Oct. 27, read 1858, Nov. 1.
" 49. 4th   "   " 1854, Oct. 14, read 1854, Sept. 14.
" 52. 1st   "   " 1855, June 5, read 1855, June 4.
" 56. Before last paragraph but one ———, ———, read 1857, Oct. 19.
" 63. 5th marginal date for 1861, June 21, read 1861, June 24.
" 66. 1st   "   " 1838, Dec. 1, read 1858, Feb. 1.
" 75. Before last paragraph but one ———, ———, read 1830, Mar. 21.
" 89. 3d marginal date for 1863, April 1, read 1863, April 6.
" 111. 4th   "   " 1858, June 2, read 1858, June 21.
" 112. 3d   "   " 1832, Nov. 11, read 1839, Nov. 11.
" 117. 3d   "   " 1823, Nov. 8, read 1823, Nov. 3.
" 118. 1st   "   " 1833, April 2, read 1832, April 2.
" 121. 4th   "   " 1850, Oct. 2, read 1854, Oct. 2.
" 123. 2d   "   " 1853, Nov. 1, read 1853, Nov. 21.
" 126. 1st   "   " 1820, Sept. 20, read 1820, Sept. 4.
" 126. 2d   "   " 1820, June 4, read 1821, June 4.
" 144. 4th   "   " 1842, Jan. 6, read 1842, June 6, and
Also, in text, same, "   " Jan. 6, read June 6.
Page 146. 3d   "   " 1860, Nov. 3, read 1860, Nov. 5.
" 151. 2d   "   " 1858, March 8, read 1858, March 1.
" 153. 1st   "   " 1860, Nov. 5, read 1860, Oct. 1.
" 153. 4th   "   " 1857, June 5, read 1857, June 22.
" 166. 3d line from bottom for page 21, read page 7.

INDEX.

	PAGE
Accumulating fund, amount set apart for	13
" " award to College Place extension	13
Admission, requirements for entering freshman class	14
Appropriation, cases for prof. Peck's room	14
" department mining engineering	15
" for furniture	15
" additional physics	15
" sports and games	15
" for 1869-70	15
" athletic sports	16
" $80 to be paid Mr. Cummings	16
" for 1870-71	16
" supplies, special appropriation	17
" cases, School of Mines, special appropriation	17
" special appropriation, repairs School of Mines and College	18
" " " repairs, Janitor's house	18
" $200 advanced for purchases in department of Geology, School of Mines	18
" Department of Physics	18
" $1,500 added to appropriation for supplies	18
" balances on hand to be added to appropriation for next year	19
" for repairs	20
" safe to be bought	20
" amendment to ordnance, appropriation to applied chemistry	20
" to applied chemistry for 1871	20
" purchase carpet Trustees' room	21
" $600 for safe	21
" President to be reimbursed $50	21
" $150, repairs for the School of Mines	21
" $225.24 appropriated for deficiency in School of Mines	21
" $150 applied for tables in School of Mines	21
" Babcock's fire extinguishers	21
" bill of Mr. Muller to be paid	22
" bill of J. W. Queen & Co. be paid	22
" $300 appropriated for English, classical and mathematical departments	22
" $175, appropriated for gas fixtures in School of Mines	22
" bill of A. T. Stewart & Co.	22
" appropriations passed and laid over	22
" supplies	22
" room for mathematical teacher in School of Mines	23
" repairs in School of Mines	23
Attendance, excused from daily attendance	23

INDEX.

	PAGE
College discipline, students not to go out	23
Commencements, and exhibitions, appropriation for commencement	24
" " expenses of	24
" " commencement	24
Department of chemistry, hour allowed to professor Joy	24
" " leave to professor Joy to rent his house	24
Degrees, to be conferred	25
Diplomas, law diplomas	25
Examinations, composition to be taken into account in determining standing..	25
" report of committee on statutes	26
" senior class examination competition	26
" honors to present senior class	27
" honors	27
" honor examinations in junior, sophomore and freshman classes	27
Fees, A. W. Frazer's case	27, 28
" Mr. Byrne, Gen. J. H. Bell	28
" refunded to F. S. Jones	28
" to refund fee to L. K. Miller	28
" tuition fee of Frank Storrs	28
" fee F. P. Pryor to be returned	29
" fee refunded to J. Constable	29
" Mr. Aymar's fee for drawing to be refunded	29
Fellowships,	29, 30
" fellows not to engage in business	30
" fellows may attend lectures without charge	30
Financial policy, permanent, unexpended balances	30
Gebhard fund	31
Herbarium	32
Instruction, committee on course of, conservation of force and connection of science transferred	33
" " " quantitative blowpipe	33
" " " civil engineering	33, 34
" " " french and german	33, 34
" " " instruction in the evidences	34
" " " instruction in french and german in the School of Mines	34
" " " special course	34
" " " instruction in french and german	35
" " " evidences, Rev. W. A. McVickar	35
" " " to report on engagement of prof. Raymond	36
" " " referred to committee in relation to assistants to professors	36
" " " chairman, committee on course	36
" " " assistant in mineralogy and metallurgy	36
" " " attendance for practice in chemistry	36
" " " instruction in chemistry referred to Committee on School of Mines	37

INDEX.

	PAGE
Instruction, committee on course of, report and resolution of Committee on School of Mines	37
" " " assistant in mathematics, School of Mines	38
Library, committee on the union of libraries of College and School of Mines	39
" " " report of joint committee of library and School of Mines	39
Miscellaneous, overflow from prof. Joy's laboratory	39
President of the, president relieved from instruction	40
Observatory, astronomical, appropriation of $1,500 for telescope	40
" " building for telescope	40
" " assistant in the observatory	40
" " Mr. Waldo appointed	40
" " $100 appropriated to furnish his room	41
" " $1,000 appropriated to Mr. Waldo	41
Meteorological observations discontinued	41
Printing, thanks to Dr. Drisler	41
" copies of Dr. Drisler's address	41
" laws, etc., affecting college	41
" new edition statutes to be printed	42
" paper on "metric system" to be printed	42
" general catalogue	42
Prize scholarships and prizes, examining committee on the greek prizes	42
" " " scholarships and fellowships	42
" " " payment of scholarships and fellowships	43
" " " prizes in english	43
" " " prizes in english amended	43
Professorships and professors, resolution on Dr. McVickar's death	44
" " " leave of absence to prof. Schmidt	45
" " " prof. Nairne's leave of absence	45
" " " resolution of french and german laid on table, and afterwards passed	45
" " " evidences	46
" " " professor of french and german	46
" " " to teach in college if required	46
" " " title of professor of mechanics	46
" " " resolution about instruction in french, prof. Loiseau	46
" " " prof. De Ternos the same	47
" " " leave of absence to prof. Newberry	47
" " " lecture by prof B. W. Hawkins	47
" " " leave of absence to prof. Drisler	47
" " " instruction in his absence	47
" " " adjunct professor of literature	47
" " " leave of absence to prof. Egleston	48
" " " committee to confer with prof. Egleston	48
" " " leave of absence to prof. Egleston	49
" " " prof. Van Amringe	49
" " " prof. Egleston to be provided for	49

	PAGE
Repairs, alterations in college buildings	50
" to college and president's house	50
" bill for professor Peck's room to be paid	50
" $30, for college and janitor's house	51
Rowing, resolution about boat club referred to standing committee	51
" $1,000 appropriated	52
Salaries, Mr. Rennell	52
" executors of Dr. McVicar	52
" increase of salaries in the college	52, 54, 55, 57, 58
" " School of Mines	53, 54, 55, 56, 57
" A. C. Merriam, salary	53
" Weeks' allowance	53, 55
" prof. Van Amringe's salary	53
" payment to prof. Lamoroux	54
" of assistant in geology and mineralogy raised	54
" janitor's salary increased this year	55
" prof. Joy's assistant	56
" salary of tutors referred to committee on course	56
" Mr. Blossom's case referred to standing committee	56
" prof. Lieber's salary to be paid to November 15	56
" $200 to Mr. Weeks	57
" treasurer to have a clerk	58
Scholarships free	58
Seal	6, 59
Site, committee on the	59, 60
" " title to the Wheelock property	61
" " enlarged accommodations referred to	61
" " $150,000 appropriated to improve the college buildings	61
Statutes, committee on the, special committee on statutes	62
" " " communication from seniors	62
" " " report of committee on the statutes	62, 67
" " " discipline	62
" " " as to scholarship	63, 64
" " " modification of programme of instruction	65
" " " order of studies, optional studies	65
" " " examinations	66
" " " attendance	66
" " " printed copies of resolutions	67
" " " voluntary studies	67
" " " chapter 3 of the statutes amended	67
" " " statute about examinations referred to	67
Standing committee, lot 111, 48th street	68
" " authority to clerk	68
" " rents unpaid for over six months	68
" " resolution on judgment in case of lot 135, 49th street	68
" " new lease of lot 300 Murray street	68
" " rents unpaid	69

INDEX.

	PAGE
Standing committee, U. S. stocks	69
" " application S. R. Van Duzer, S. A. Buckley and E. C. Crocker	69
" " leases of lots	69
" " application presbyterian church	70
" " leases	70
" " alterations president's house	70
" " lease to J. & T. Stevenson	70
" " lease of 37 Lafayette place	70
" " party wall, lots 109 and 110	70
" " Dr. Trenor's lease	71
" " leases of lots	71
" " power to committee	71
" " application of Mercer street church	71, 72
" " leases of lots in upper estate	72
" " widening of Robinson street	72
" " application of Mr. A. Higgins	72
" " lease of No. 37 Lafayette place to be sealed	73
" " S. Mason, application for license to make soap referred	73
" " renewal of down-town leases referred to	73
" " authorized to commence suits	73
" " Mr. Hagadorn and others, application declined	74
" " leases, Greenwich street lots	74
" " leases, lots iv. and vii	74
" " paving Madison avenue and 50th street	74
" " Mrs. Vanderpoel and Mrs. McLanahan, leases, &c.	75
" " lots 308 and 309 Greenwich street	75
" " overflow in wing of college	75
" " reduction of fees referred to	76
" " renewal of leases	76
" " to inquire about making contributions to Sewannee University	77
" " to appoint appraisers	77
" " lease of lot 179 Barclay street	77
" " painting the college buildings	77
" " representation at Vienna exposition	78
" " leases in Barclay street	78
" " painting and repairing the college	78
" " to direct repairs in the college	78
" " not to paint	78
" " contract with Joseph D. Beers	79
" " new leases in Barclay street	79
" " advances to the Dean of the School of Mines	79
" " Mr. Waldo's salary	79
Students, Dr. C. A. Bacon's case	80
" W. L. Murphy's case	80
" C. C. Merriam to attend prof. Rood in college	80
" Mr. A. F. Smith's application granted	80

INDEX.

	PAGE
Treasurer, U. S. certificates	80
" certified copy of preceding resolution	81
" authorization of treasurer to employ attorney	81
" profs. Chandler and Newbury, Ives case	81
" appropriation advanced to prof. Egleston	81
" payment of college bonds	81
" investments by treasurer	82
" Mr. Kemble's portrait	82
" leave of absence	82
" acting treasurer	82
" $400 to prof. Egleston for School of Mines library	83
" power of attorney to collect interest on U. S. stock	83
" authority to collect N. Y. interest	83
" pavement 50th street	83
" grant to city corporation	84
" bond to be assigned to Miss Gelston	84
" commutation Rhinelander rents	84
" instructed, Gebhard professor	85
" payment for ball-ground for sophomores and freshmen	85
" Dr. Moore's annuity	85
" power to sell stock	85
" clerk to furnish copy of the preceding resolution	86
" to receive awards for land taken	86
Trustees, meetings called by chairman	86
" matriculation book discovered, thanks to Dr. Francis	86
" prof. Adrain's portait	87
" resignation of Mr. Fish	87
" donation to the library, thanks to the Rev. Dr. Brown	88
" " " " thanks to Messrs. McMillan	88
" proposed association with Cooper Union, committee to confer	88
" death of Mr. Jones	89
" Dr. Torrey's house	89
" request of Mr. Rutherfurd to withdraw his resignation	89
" death of Dr. Torrey, resolutions thereon	89
" use of Dr. Torrey's house offered to his daughters	90
" portrait of Dr. Torrey	91
Tutorships, tutor in english department	91
" tutorship in rhetoric	91
School of mines, fees	92
" " foreign exchange	92
" " admission	93
" " free tuition, privileges to students	93
" " " notes of students	93
" " scholarships, notice of motion to amend statute of School of Mines	94
" " salaries	94
" " authority to raise funds, donations requested	94
" " Smithsonian minerals	94

INDEX.

	PAGE
School of Mines, geological collection, insurance of geology and paleontology collection...	95
" " " " Dr. Newberry's collection...	95
" " " " second reading of Dr. Newberry's collection...	95
" " laboratories, blow-pipe laboratory, referred to standing committee...	96
" " " $150 appropriated for tables for prof. Egleston.	96
" " assistants, assistant in college and School of Mines...	96
" " " honorary assistants...	96
" " students, $25 to be paid to Mr. Alfred Barnard...	97
" " " application of Schuyler Hamilton granted...	97
" " " leave to Mr. José Aymar to take drawing lessons..	97
" " " " Messrs. Buckley and Storrs to take drawing lessons...	97
" " printing, article on mining engineering to be printed...	97
" " purchase of meteorites, application of prof. Egleston for $100 declined...	27
" " suspension of exercises...	98
" " by-laws, age of admission...	98
" " instruction in french and german...	98
" " degree of Ph. D. referred to committee, School of Mines...	99
" " donations...	100
Law school, annual sermon at...	102
" stated meeting...	102
" accommodation for...	102
" duplicate law diplomas...	103
" addresses at commencement...	103
" committee to provide accommodations...	103
" thanks to Messrs. Roelker, Curtis and Wetmore...	103
" " " Messrs. Strong, Parsons and Wright...	103
" " " Dr. Morgan...	104
" warden to regulate the election of valedictorian...	104
" Rev. Dr. Potter's sermon...	104
" Bishop Potter's sermon...	104
" memorial of prof. Lieber...	104
" Mr. Bidwell...	104
" building and maintenance of, referred to law committee...	105
" Dr. Lieber...	105
" warden to have charge of the new law school...	106
" assistant professor...	107
" compensation...	107, 109
" third year, adjunct professor...	107
" Mr. Austin Abbott, adjunct professor of municipal law...	107
" instruction in Dr. Lieber's department referred to law committee	107
" LL. B. to be conferred...	108
" Dr. Lieber's professorship...	108
" instruction, faculty...	109

INDEX.

	PAGE
Law school, expenditures, $250 appropriated to ventilation	109
" " bill of 608.29 for repairs	109
" " Mr. Randolph's fee to be refunded	109
" " $300 appropriated for commencement	110
" " lease of Mr. Schermerhorn's house for	110
" " $300 appropriated for removal of	110
" " rent of school for May	110
" prizes, prizes in departments of constitutional history and public law	110
" " report, law committee to extend prize in department public law, &c., another year	111
" " with power to extend it to second year	111
" " thanks to the committee on prizes	111
" degrees, B. A., LL. B.	112
School of medicine, committee on college of physicians and surgeons	112
Ordinance establishing a permanent financial policy	113
Errata	118

Printed in Dunstable, United Kingdom